W9-CZS-800

Karen Barth

Archivist, Curator, and
Project Manager: Kelly Worman

Photography: Jason Wyche

Catalogue produced and edited by
Georgia Marsh

Design by The Graphics Office

# Light and Fog: The Paintings of Karen Barth

Tom Huhn

Barth's paintings likewise suspend the viewer between residual layers of image and process, and thereby bring to the fore an experience that alternates between restfulness and quickening, between stasis and dynamism.

It's important to understand and to appreciate how this last body of Karen Barth's work came into existence, as well as the precise form of existence it now takes. There is a surprising kinship between the process by which these works were made and the multiply-determined experiences of suspension that they prompt. The works began as small paintings, their dimensions varying from approximately 8" x 10" to 14" x 18". Barth began by painting a smaller version of each work that could then be expanded and (re)produced as a digital print in the size that she envisioned the original painting should have. Recalling the relationship in sculpture between a maquette and its intended destination as a fully realized object, I'm inclined to use the term maquette. Maquette is commonly used to describe the initial object in a sculptural process whereby the artist produces a reduced scale object to serve as the source for the fabrication of a larger realization of it. These smaller pieces by Barth, in addition to being paintings in their own right, serve as source and model for the larger objects which, though digitally produced, Barth insisted were also in fact paintings. Barth worked assiduously to produce the highest quality digital prints possible, often repeatedly color-correcting each print until she was satisfied that it matched the source painting. What we are viewing in the exhibition is the paintings in the scale and size and colors as Barth envisioned and produced them. What is so noteworthy and unusual is that these works arrive at their final state of existence as paintings in a procedure unlike any other paintings I am familiar with.

Spending time amidst Barth's final suite of 24 paintings is to find oneself deeply submerged in many of the most compelling issues in the practices of contemporary painting. Barth's paintings likewise suspend the viewer between

pages 4-6
*White Light* (detail)
2014
Archival pigment on paper, mounted on panel, 40" x 30"

residual layers of image and process, and thereby bring to the fore an experience that alternates between restfulness and quickening, between stasis and dynamism. The suspension of the viewer within and between these currents is precisely what allows each of us to tarry sensuously and provocatively within the folds and flows of Barth's paintings.

A first powerful impression of this body of Barth's work signals the mobility and fleetingness of the imagery, complemented by the overall commitment to the quasi-figural elements within many of the paintings. These paintings appear of a piece with one another and so too point to a world utterly consistent in—and full of—colors and textures. The works point to and evoke a world; they stand as ciphers for a world beyond us while being at the same time oddly familiar. In this regard one imagines the paintings as a merger, the twinned products of conviction and hesitation. Their conviction seems to lie in the sheer confidence in the reality of the appearances they body forth while their hesitation resides in the very transitoriness of the imagery itself.

One visibly prominent suspension in the paintings is the alternation between abstraction and landscape. It seems Barth was well aware of the long tradition of landscape painting in which it came to express and embody a certain kind of yearning. The longing within landscape painting means that landscapes appear as a projection of what nature might look like were it wholly in accord with our feelings toward it. And yet, landscape painting is no simple projection of what we want nature to be, it is also, as yearning, an expression of a longing to be at one with nature, to be made whole by and within nature, and finally, to be reconciled with it rather than to continue as its adversary. That each of her paintings appears as a cohesive and dynamic unity—despite the dizzying variety that often spills across it—is a testament to the enduring classical goal that art is to create unity amidst variety. To put it mimetically, we might imagine that the legacy of landscape painting in Barth's work is a form of sympathetic magic, a desire to align ourselves with and in nature, to affirm at once both nature's and our own animated unities. Barth's work is no mere appropriation of what is other

[T]he legacy of landscape painting in Barth's work is a form of sympathetic magic...

than us, but rather an attempt to draw nearer to it, even to submit ourselves to it, and thus not only to transform it but more importantly to position ourselves in just the right place so that we might be transformed by it.

The productive tension in Barth's paintings, at once both visual and experiential, lies between two poles that might also be designated flow and image. We could similarly approach this tension by way of her overarching commitment to abstraction, to the process of making that actively suspends itself in a double movement: one direction is a movement away (abstraction) and the other a movement toward (image). And yet, I also suspect Barth would be somewhat dubious regarding this talk of image in paintings, and especially in reference to her paintings, since she was fiercely committed to the notion that paintings are not images, but rather things. And the particular kind of thing a painting is, includes, most obviously and straight-forwardly, that it is a material thing, which is to say that it is a thing that exists not only as matter, but more importantly as the residue of singular processes and events.

What it means not just to say but to emphasize that a painting is a material thing is to acknowledge the ways in which it resists being pulled entirely into the immaterial realm of the image, into that hovering appearance that floats above the surface of the painting. Barth's paintings suspend themselves between the materiality of paint and the ephemerality of the appearing image. I want to suggest that it is just here, in this peculiar suspension, that Barth's paintings thereby become models of human life. Here again we might note the strong presence of mimesis in Barth's practice: the digital extrapolation of these works from the original paintings mimetically parallels the practice of abstracting a painting from the experience of viewing—or of imagining—nature. By extension we might say that this artistic practice points to how we live, for to be alive is also to exist in two rather different realms, that of material embodied existence as well as that of immaterial, ephemeral thing. This ephemeral life of ours has been variously characterized as mind (in opposition to the material brain), consciousness (recall that for the Existentialists especially consciousness is not even

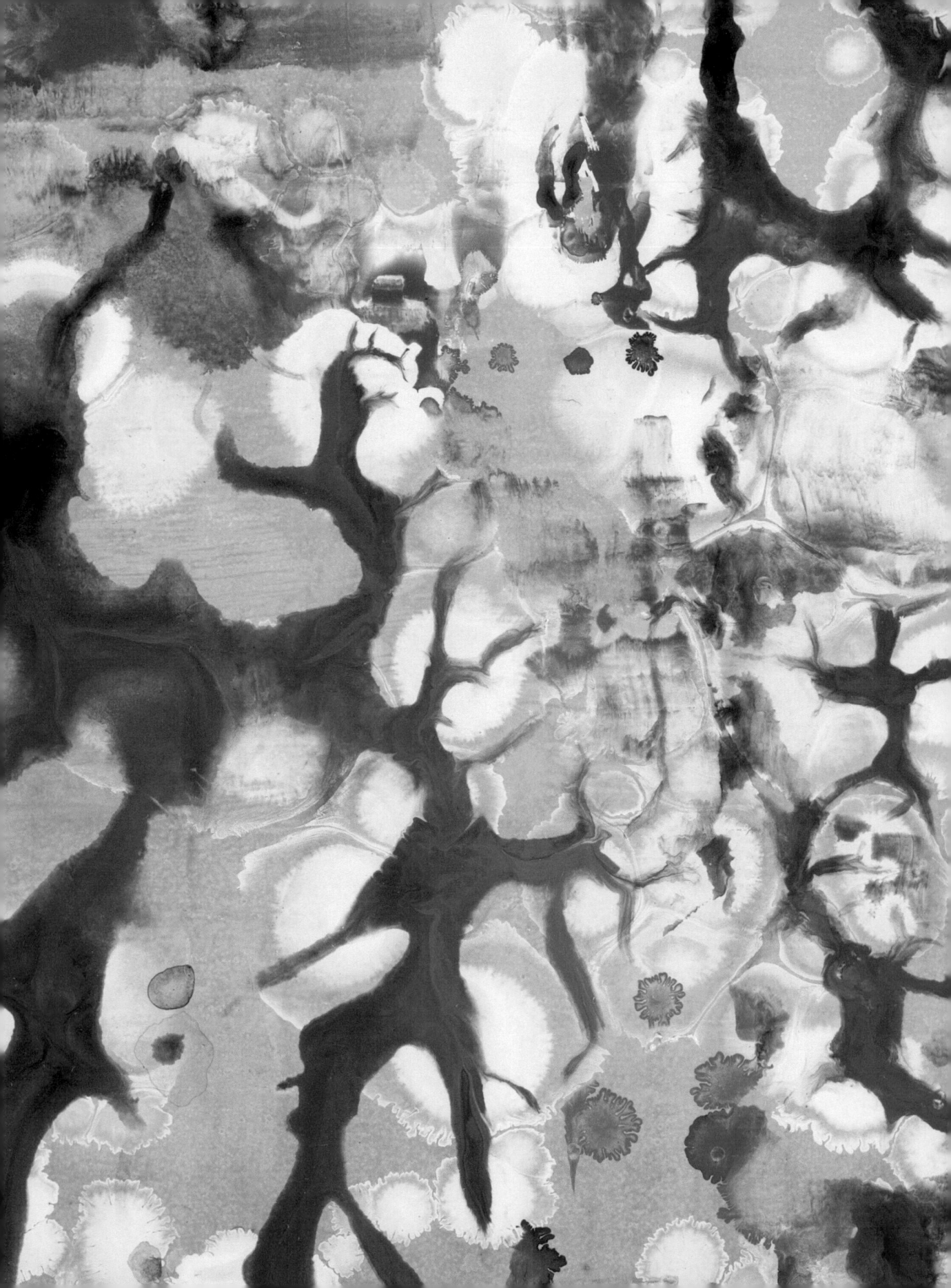

a thing but instead a mere motion; Sartre even likens it to a breeze blowing across a field), spirit, soul, etc.

Consider how this vacillating suspension between matter and evanescence occurs in the painting titled *Pond*. Imagine yourself in the position of a bird on a branch above the pond, looking down on its surface. Note first the ingenious production of a pictorial space between the base layer of the pond's surface and the layer of reflections suspended in an evanescent space floating somewhere a few feet above the pond. Consider how what I'm describing as the reflected tree branches themselves come to appear as things already melting into the texture and motion of the water below. Look too at how the selfsame branches nonetheless retain their materiality even as they deliquesce; this is a depiction and enactment of an ongoing transitional state between materiality and immateriality, between stasis and dynamism.

But so too do the branchings in many of the paintings also allude to the body, especially to its membranes and to its fluid inner coursings. It's as if Barth's paintings function both as microcosm and macrocosm, vacillating between the various allusions in which the paintings point away from us and toward, for example, the geological, while they function microcosmically in pointing toward us, indeed, inside us. This continuous dualism is one of the most sustained achievements of this body of Barth's work, that it so subtly maintains a balance between that which exceeds us and that out of which we are composed.

One way to appreciate this sustained and sustaining balance is to place the paintings *Ground Fog* and *White Light* alongside one another, and to observe how the former appears as a well of dark opacity and *White Light* its contrary. *White Light* promises nearly to efface itself in an increasing intensity of light while *Ground Fog* betokens a kind of enveloping darkness. And yet both paintings bring to light just how much there is to see within the mere ebb and flow of light. Both paintings give the impression of some rich and extensive percolating, though of what we cannot discern. They each promise to reveal something primordial about the world, to show us the origin of

*Ground Fog* (detail)
2014
Archival pigment
on paper, mounted
on panel, 48" x 36"

things, however thick and porous, vibrant and full, it might prove to be. Note even how *Ground Fog*'s congealing images complement the melting yellows of *White Light*.

One of the painters that this body of Karen's work most readily brings to mind is Charles Burchfield, whose dreamy land and skyscapes appear as precursors to Barth's more fluid evocations of field, pond, season, fog and night. And though Burchfield's fluidity is to be seen in both the visual forms themselves as well as in his famously deployed set of key allegorical motifs—in other words the fluidity also pours through the relation of icon to image—Barth's more fluid imagery and process point still more directly toward the fluid fact of being alive. Barth's subject—her activity we might say—was to depict and enact the condition of an active embodiment, of a motion and a flow unencumbered by the blockages of pain, or thought, or suffering. A painting that epitomizes this dynamic juxtaposition of rest and motion is *Spring Mist*. Consider how the title and even the hints of lavender at the top and center of the painting allude to Jackson Pollock's iconic 1950 work, *Number 1 (Lavender Mist)*—Barth was deeply moved by Pollock's achievements and so we must take these allusions seriously. It's interesting in this light to see the dark tendrils of *Spring Mist*, reaching centerward from the left and right edges of the painting, as complements to and extensions of the drips of *Lavender Mist*. "Drip" has never seemed a very accurate description of how *Lavender Mist* was made nor how it appears; this is true of *Spring Mist* as well. Better to think of Pollock and Barth both attempting to outmaneuver the constriction and conventions of the traditional line in painting. Pollock's pourings facilitated the paint to, if you will, compose its own line, to allow the paint to align itself; Barth's paintings likewise sidestep the whole problem of the drawn and painted line by giving the paint a compositional agency of its own. Where Jackson Pollock poured, Karen Barth instead allowed the paint to leak and to blossom, and thereby to flow and delineate an aliveness that inevitably exceeds us.

*Spring Mist* (detail)
2014
Archival pigment on paper, mounted on panel, 25" x 35"

**Tom Huhn** is the chair of the Art History and BFA Visual & Critical Studies Departments at the School of Visual Arts in New York City. More information can be found at tomhuhn.com.

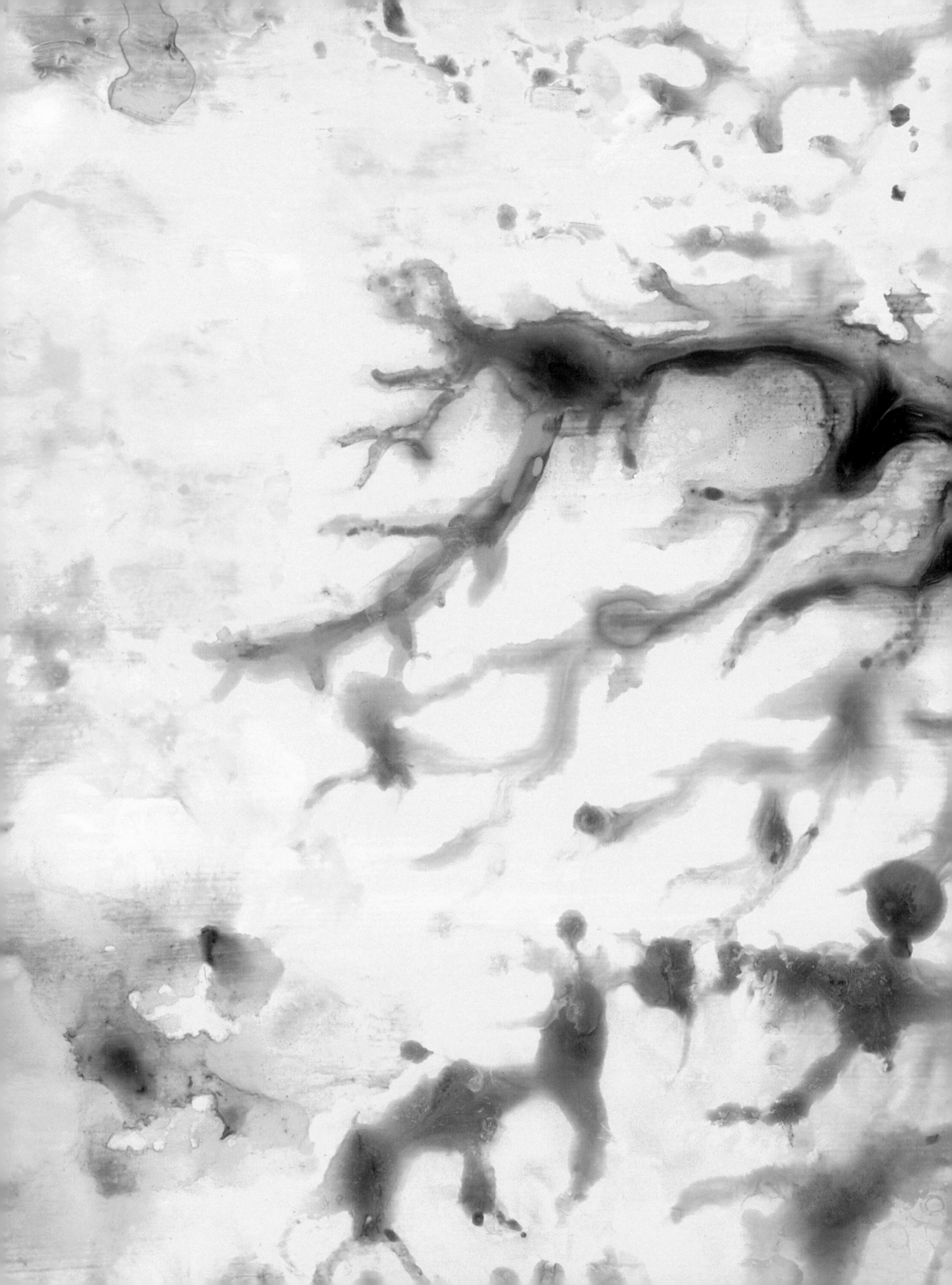

Works 2014–2015

My work is inspired by the possibility of making a painting that is abstract and self-contained, while simultaneously suggesting a relationship to nature, a painting that is unfixed, evoking changing conditions of form, light, color and atmosphere.

I begin by mixing a palette of colors that I derive from either my direct experience in nature or one mediated by a color photograph. When I start, all I know is my need to put these colors together to make a painting. I do not know what the painting will look like in advance of its making and rid my mind of any pre-conceived plan, image or technique.

I work with a vocabulary of organic processes, like puddling, staining, dripping and pulling. I have evolved this vocabulary over many years, through trial and error, to gain an understanding of how paint can behave. I paint on small panels as a way to establish intimacy with the painting and to rapidly generate new organic forms, color interactions and concurrent formal decisions, to create a balance between chaos and control, accident and intention. The resultant painting is then enlarged via a technical process that calls to mind the gesture of spreading one's fingers on a touch screen to see an image in greater detail, allowing the viewer to be both inside and outside the image, to experience intimacy on a grand scale.

My objective is to make a painting that reinvigorates the language of abstraction and forges a renewed bond to nature. What I seek is a connection to the larger world via a painting that suggests a confluence between nature, paint and technology as process and the sense of immediacy and aliveness that this fused experience provides for me.

Karen Barth

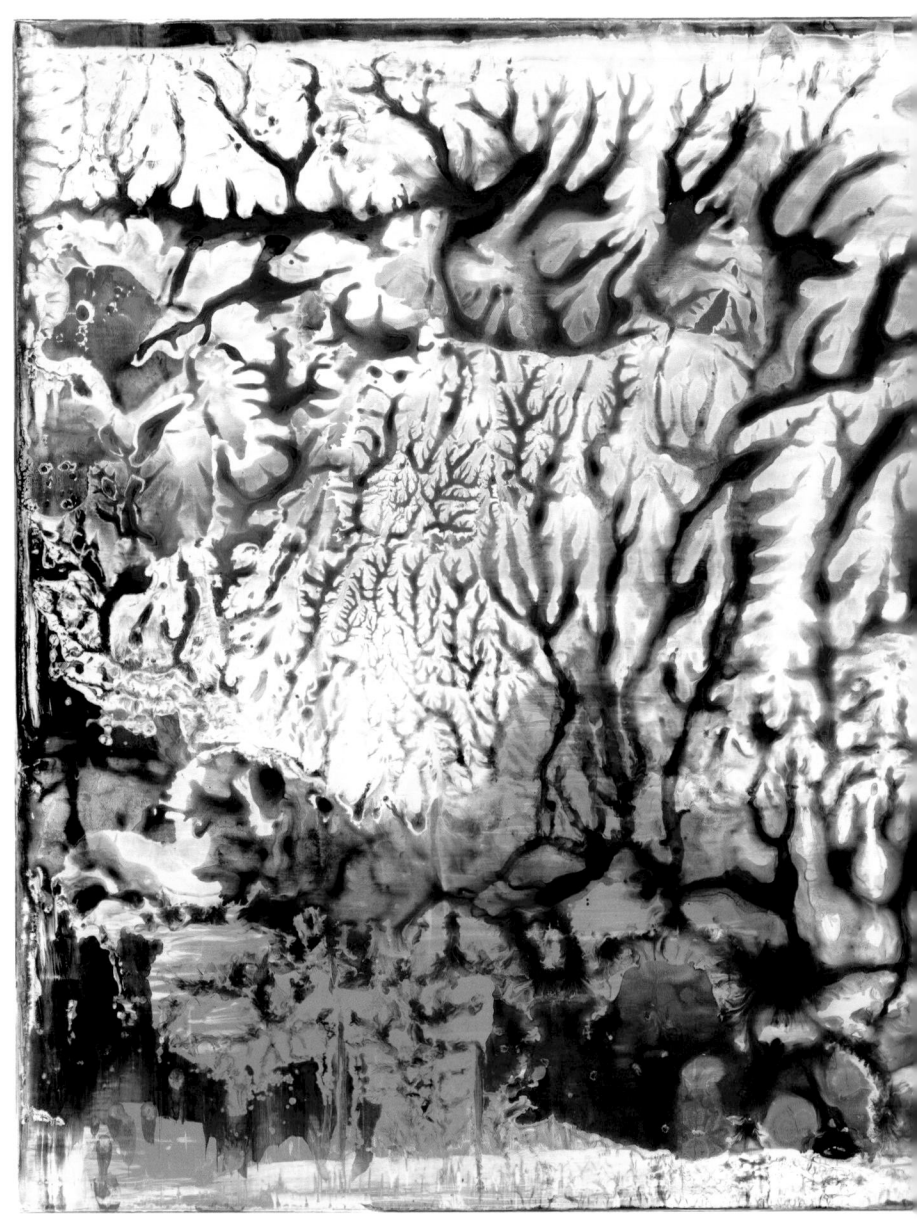

*Winter*
2014
Archival pigment
on paper, mounted
on panel, 40" x 80"

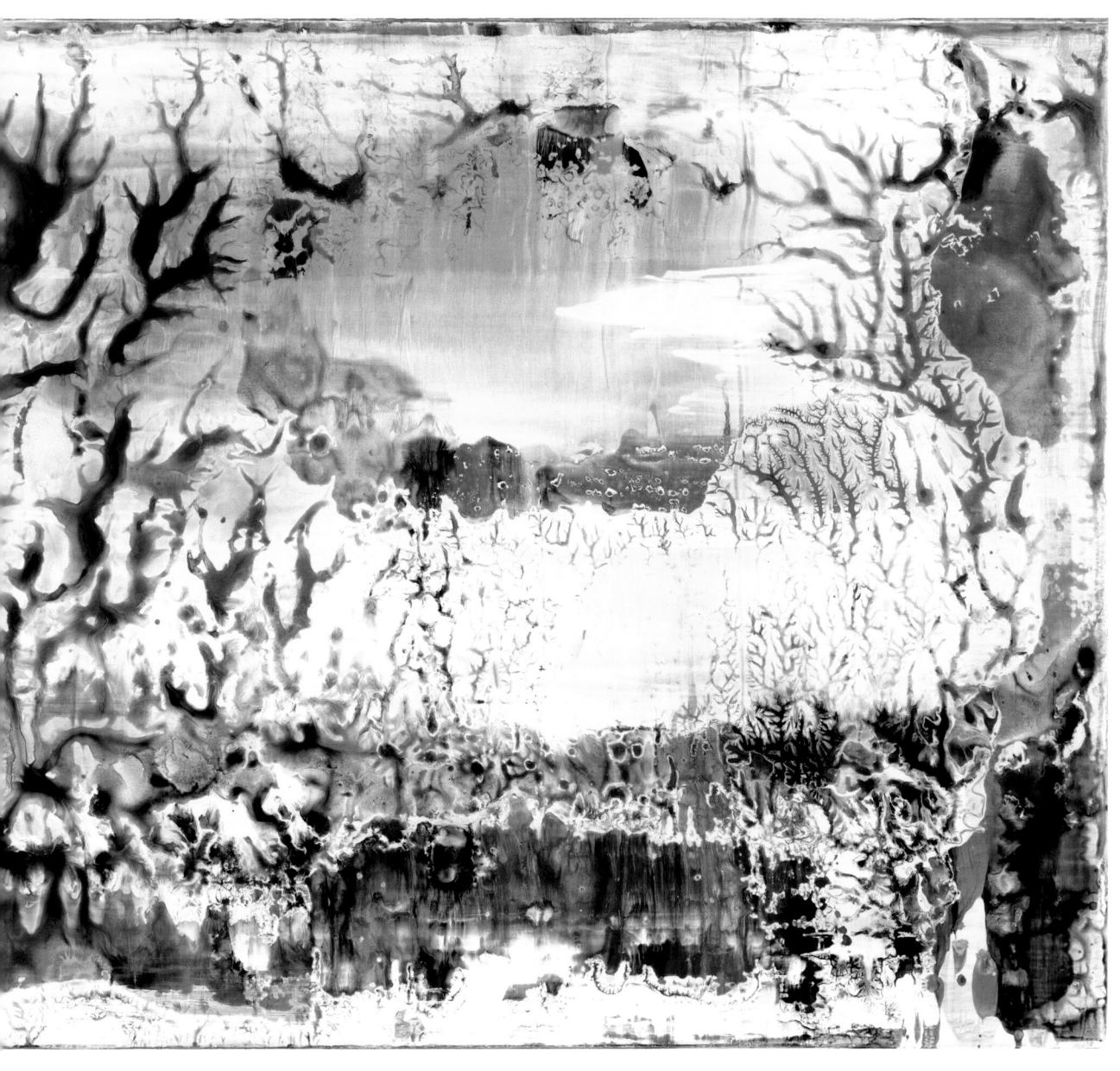

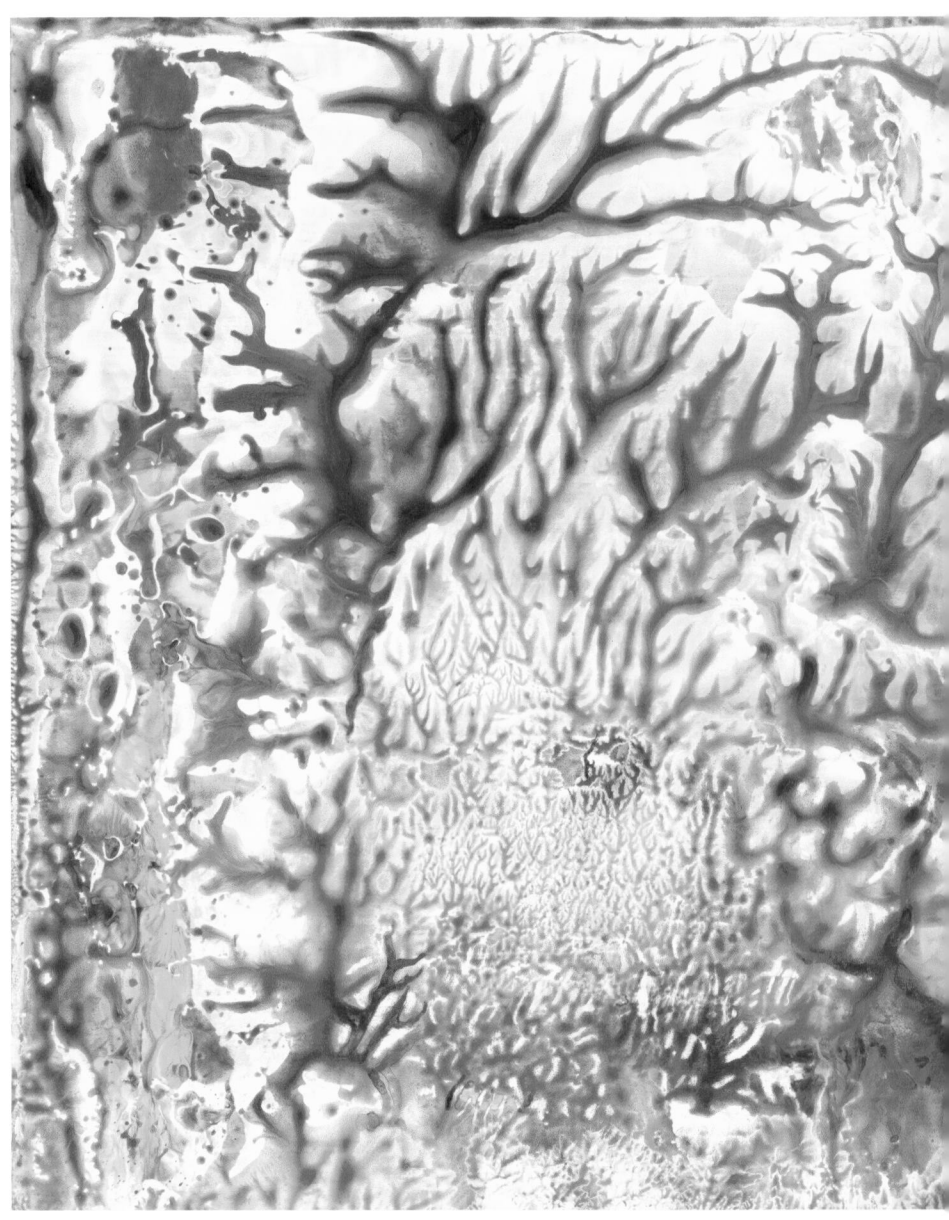

*Spring*
2014
Archival pigment
on paper, mounted
on panel, 40" x 80"

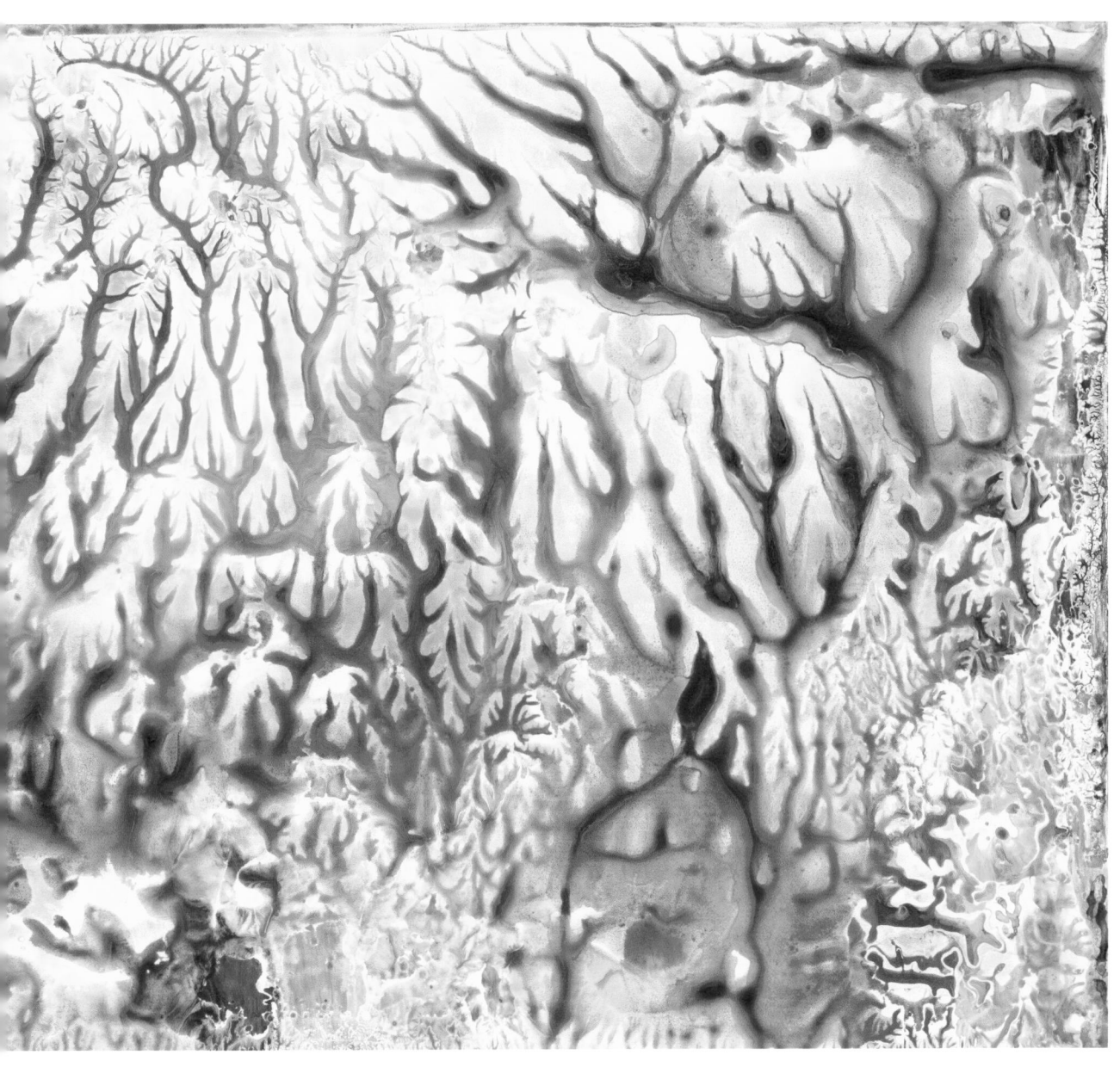

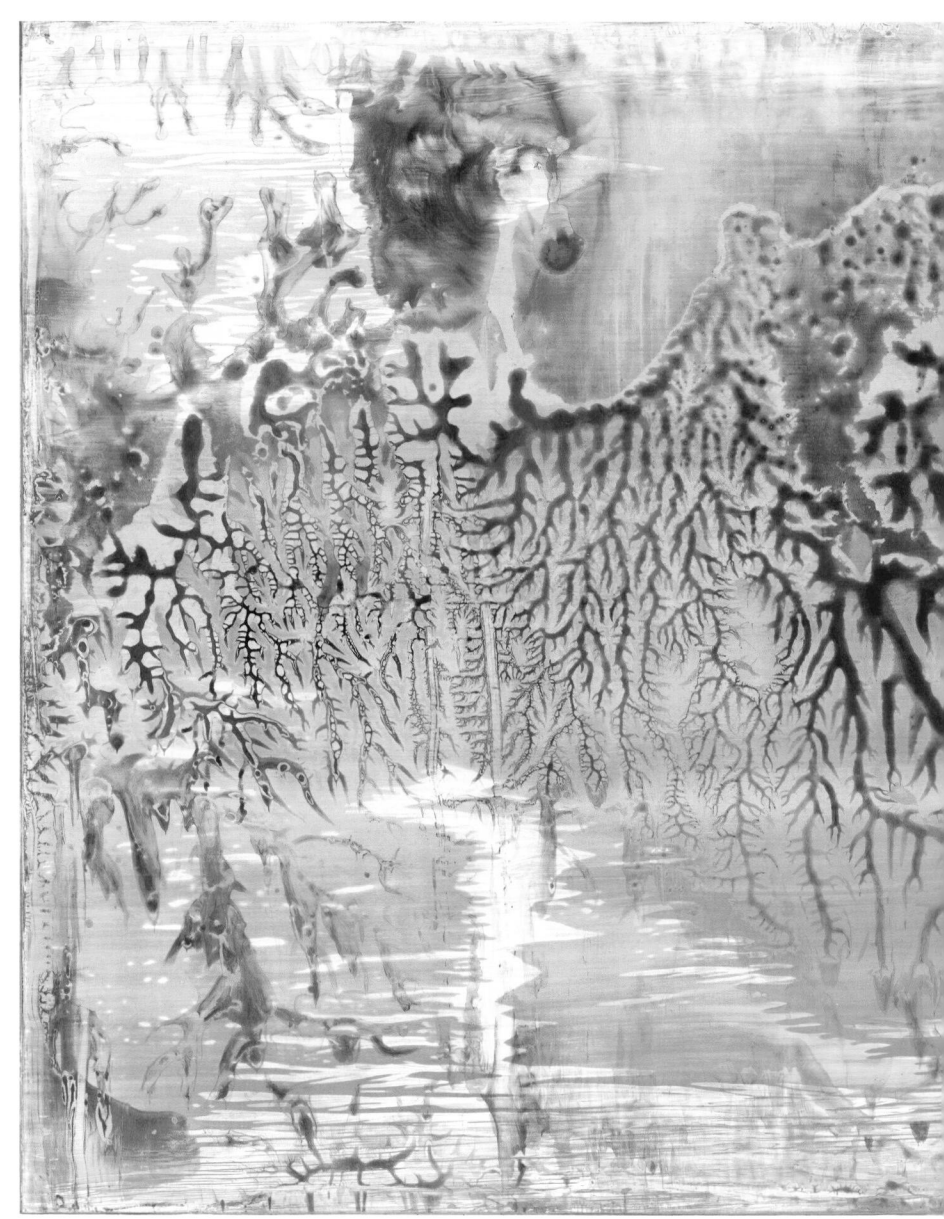

*Summer*
2014
Archival pigment
on paper, mounted
on panel, 40" x 80"

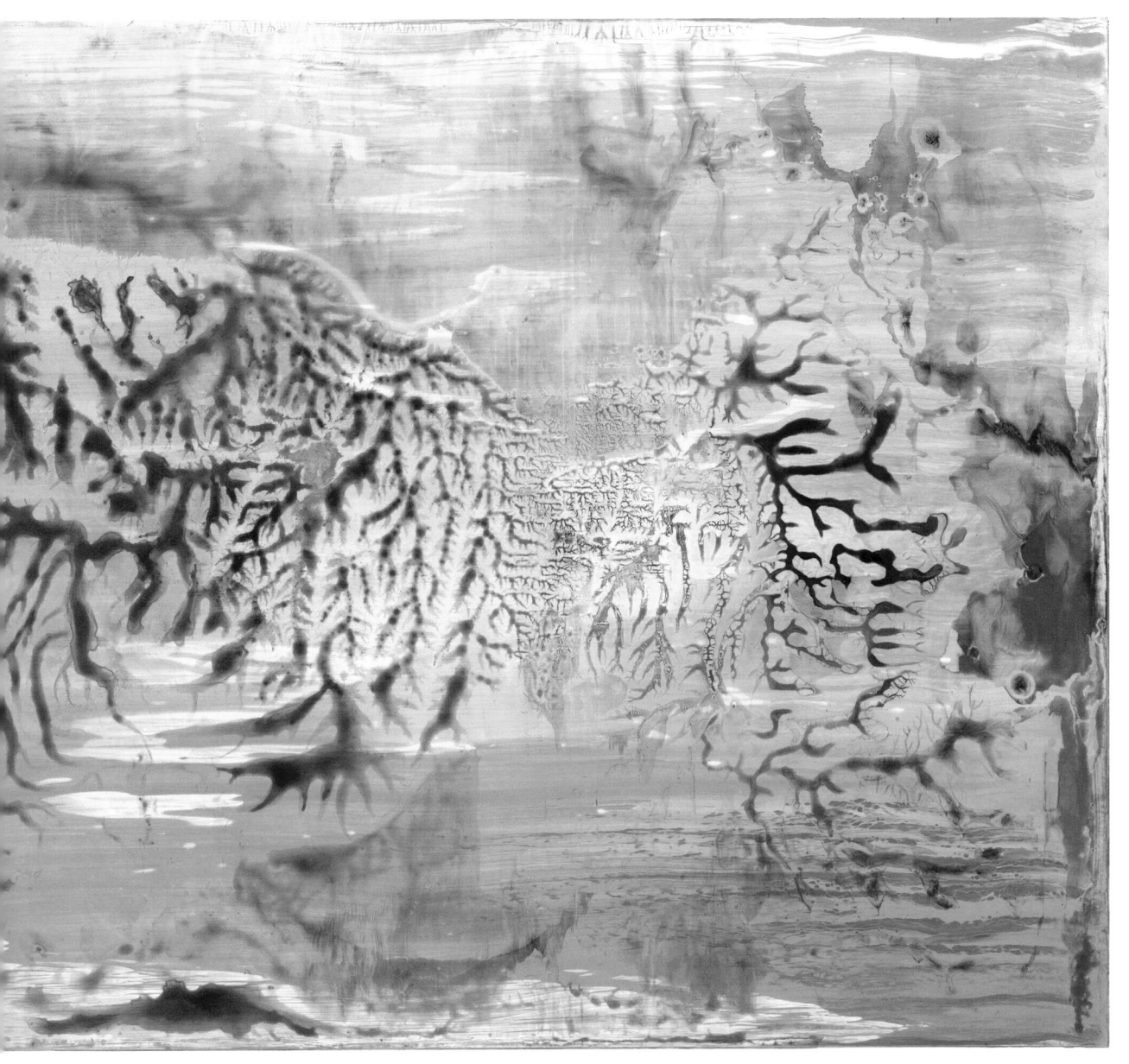

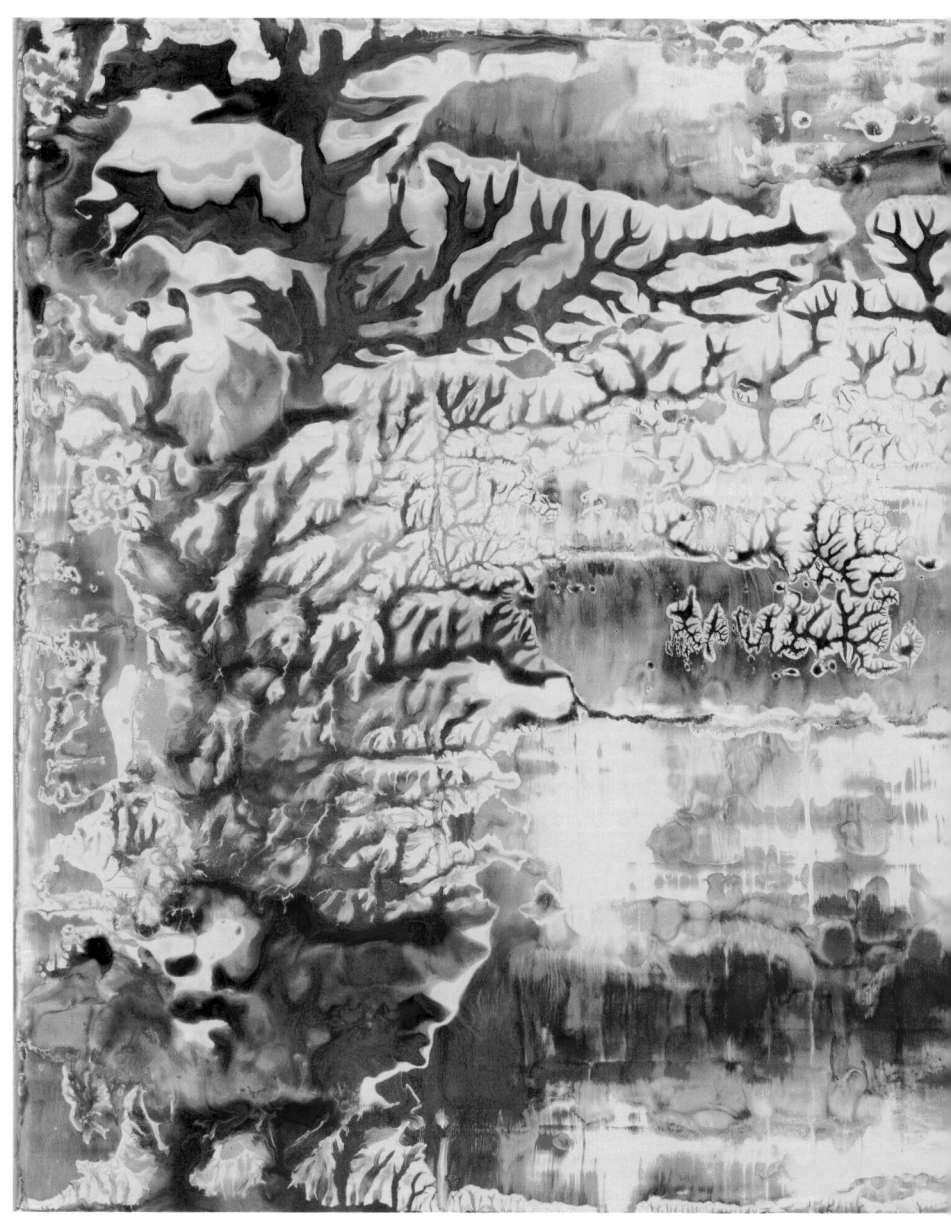

*Fall*
2014
Archival pigment
on paper, mounted
on panel, 40" x 80"

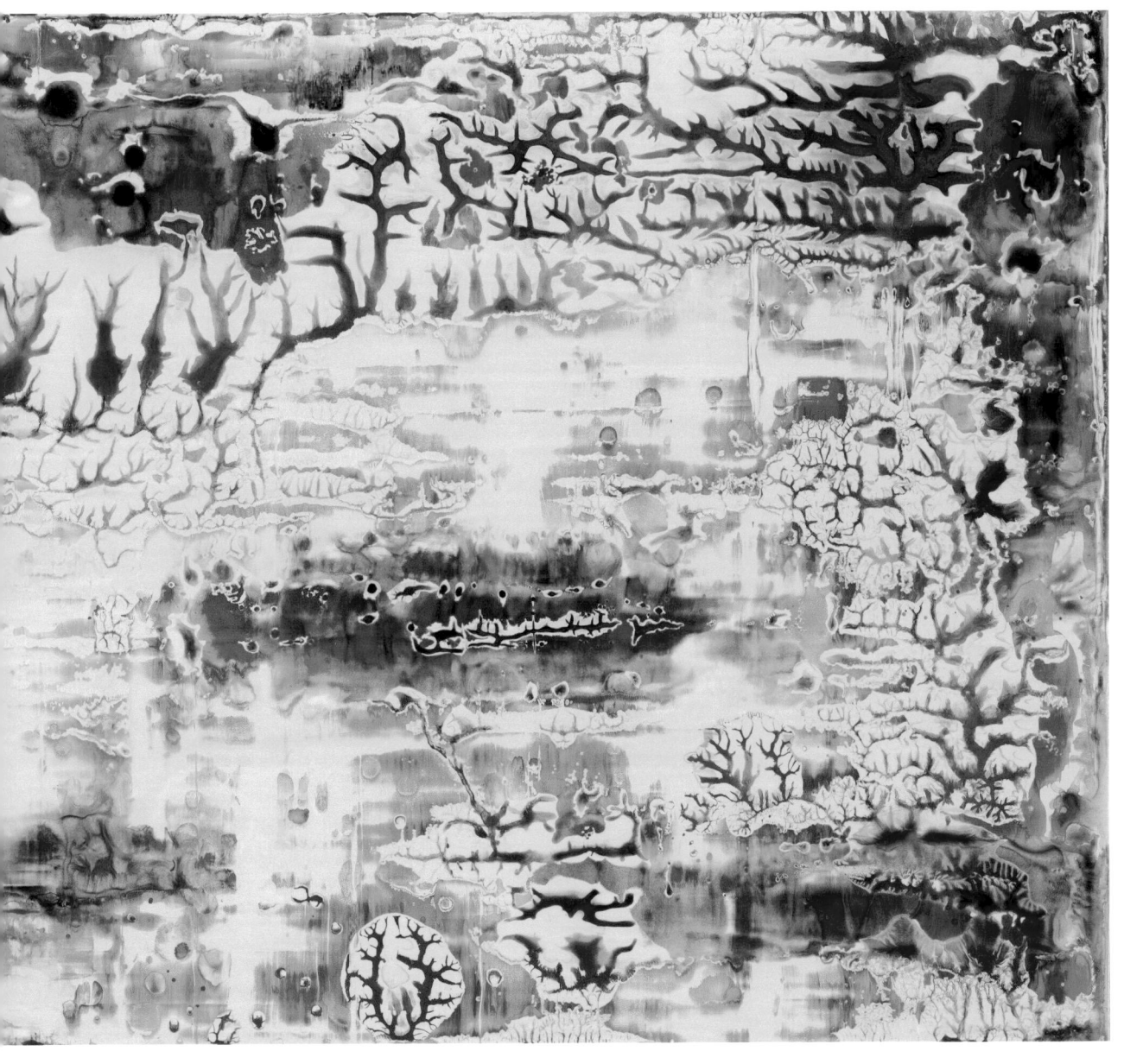

**End of Autumn**
2015
Archival pigment
on paper, mounted
on panel, 48" x 36"

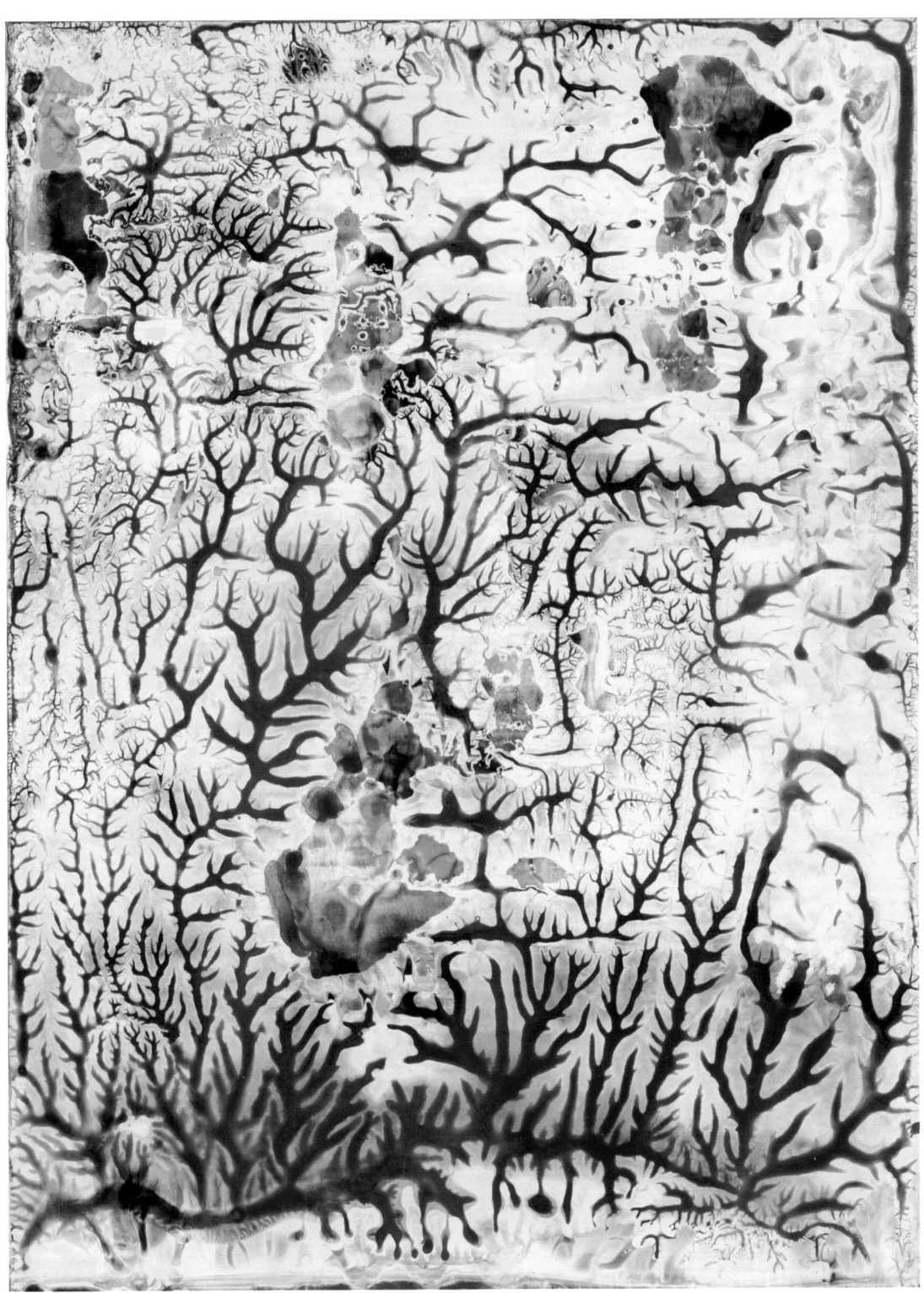

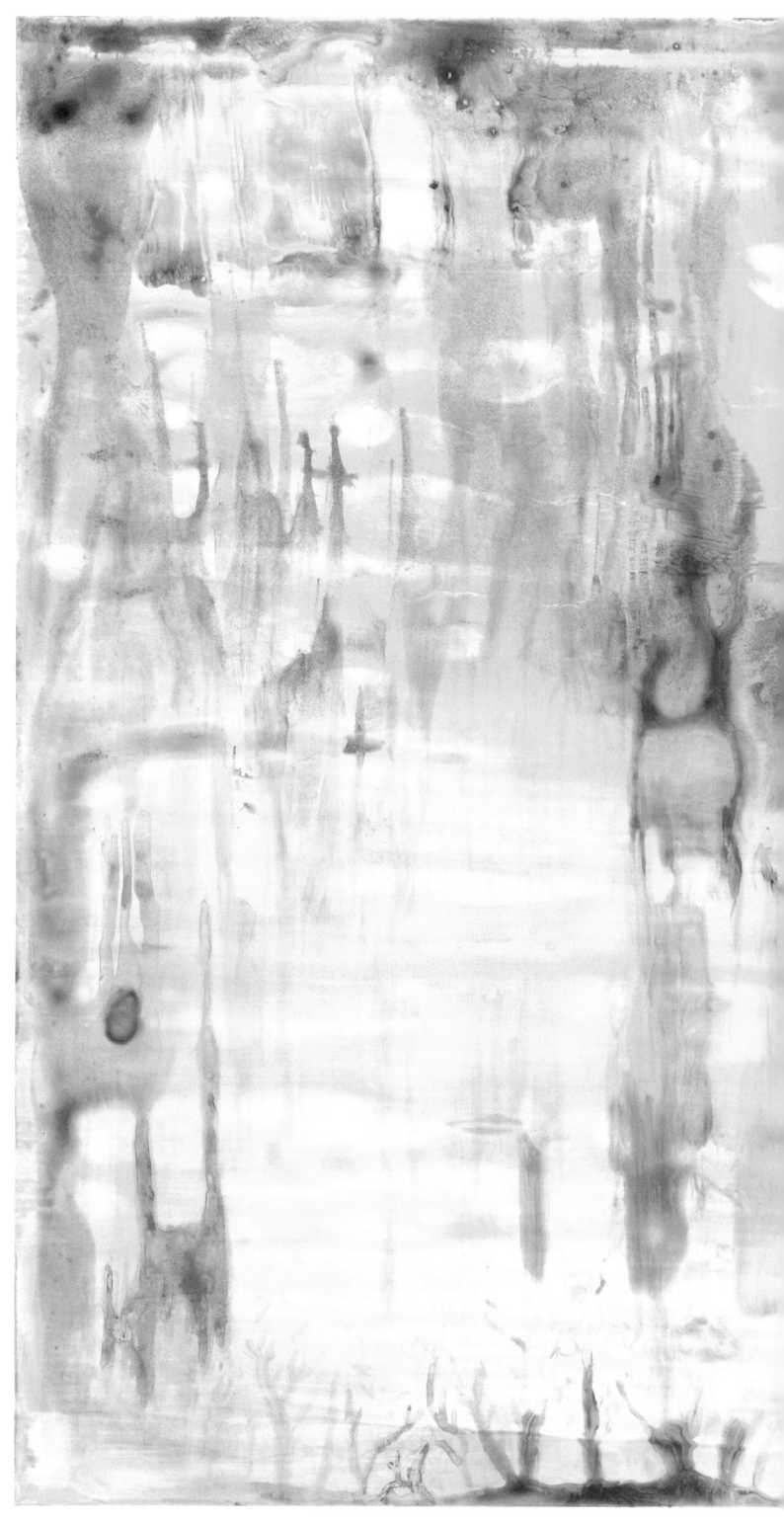

*Catskills (1)*
2014
Archival pigment
on paper, mounted
on panel, 15" x 22"

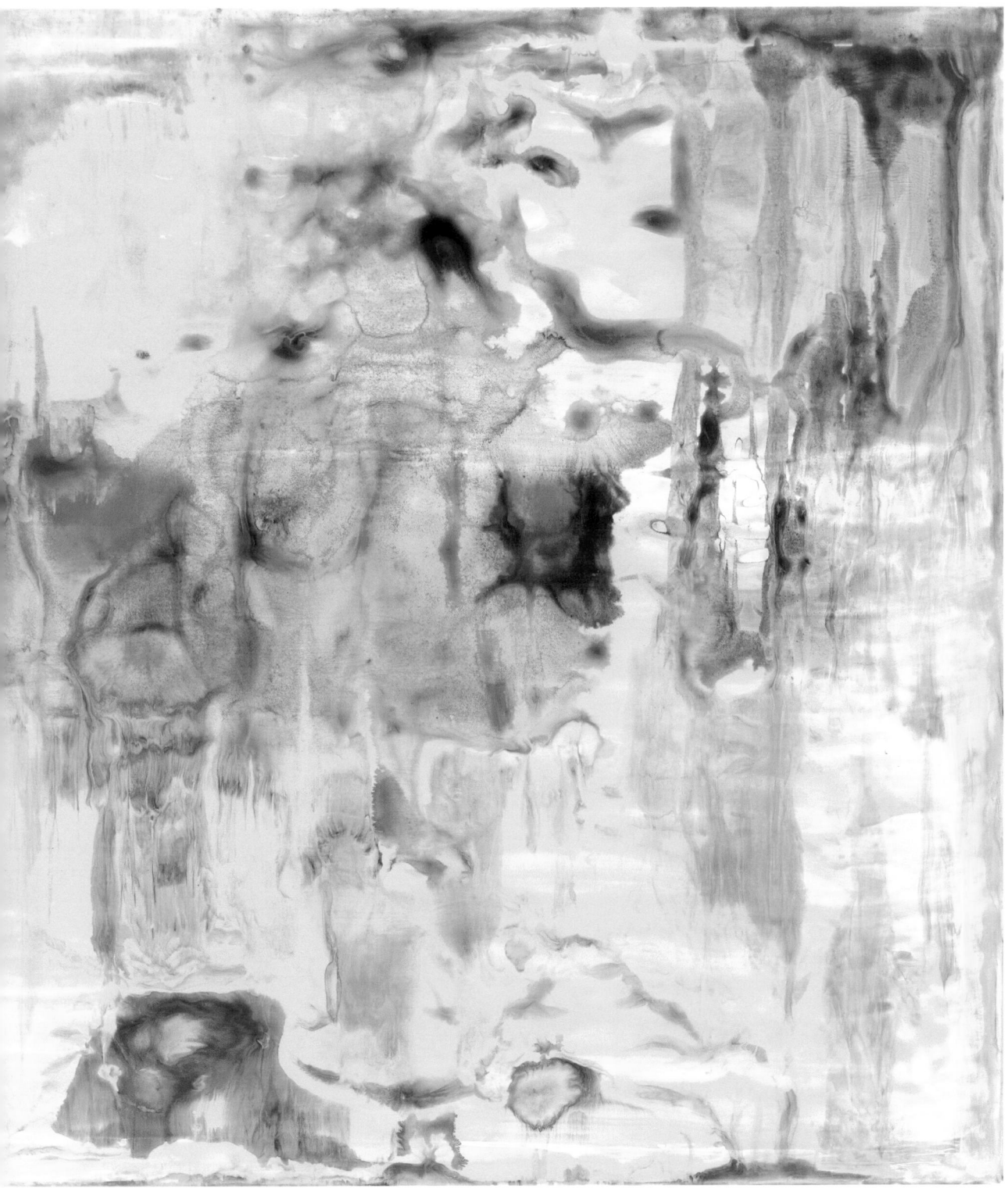

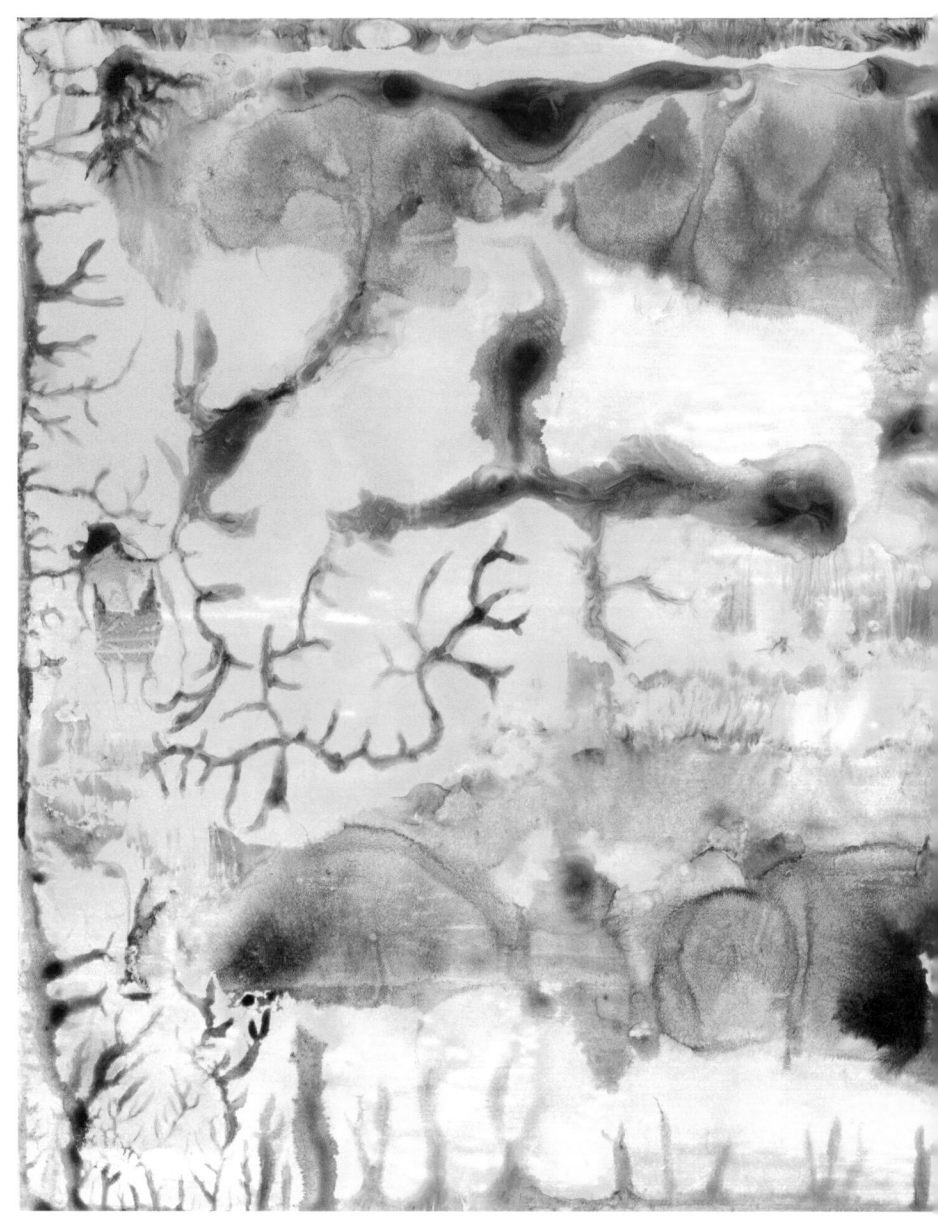

*Catskills (2)*
2014
Archival pigment
on paper, mounted
on panel, 30" x 60"

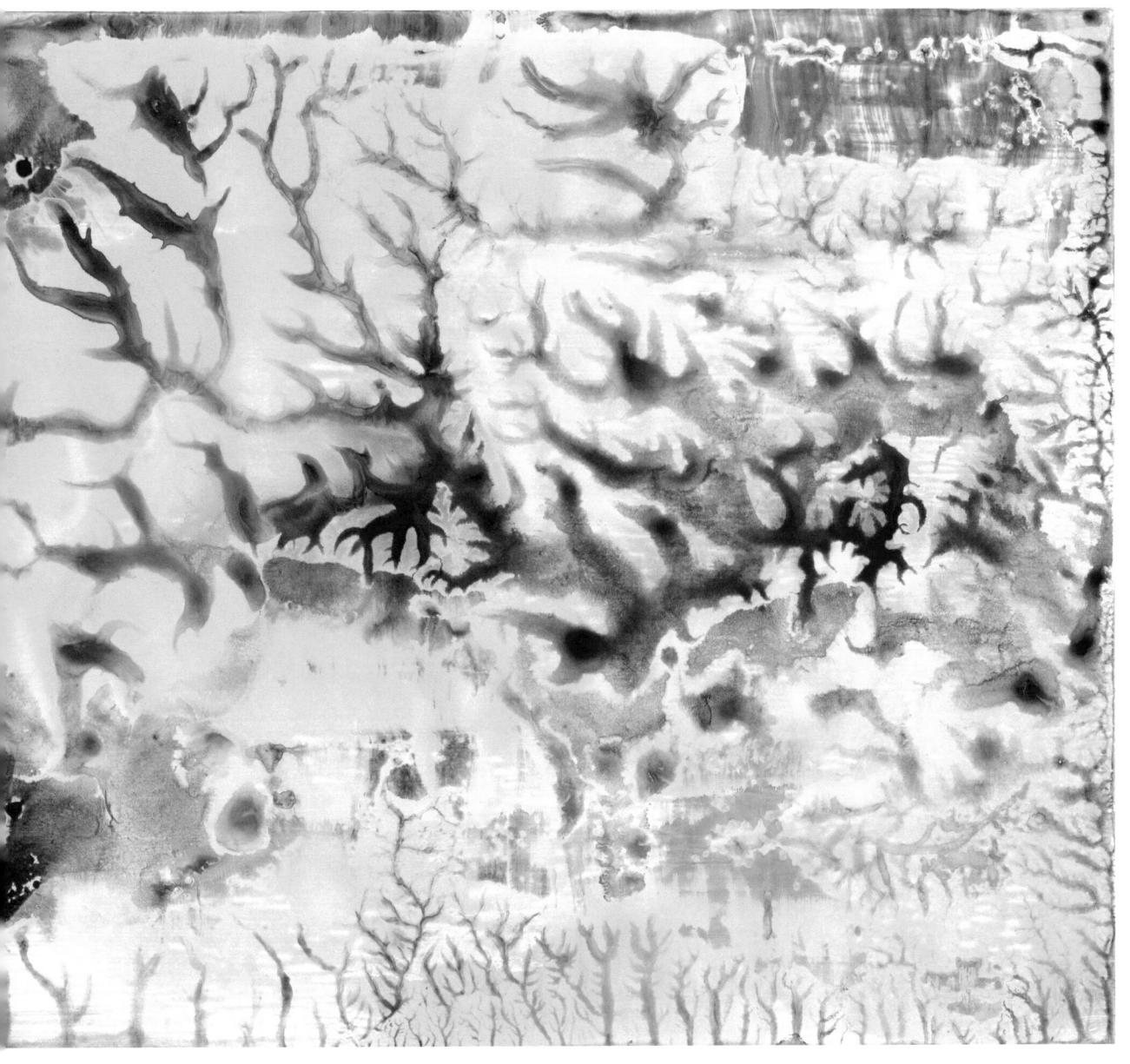

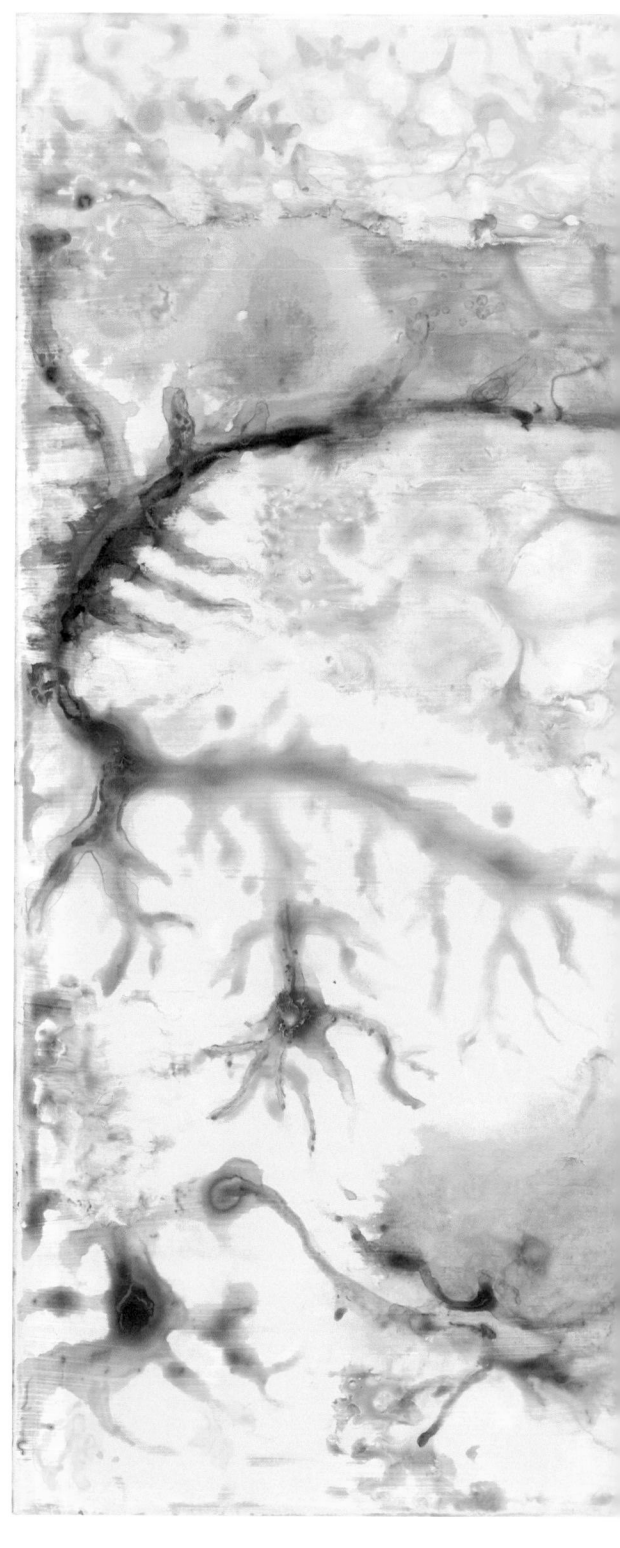

*Spring Mist*
2014
Archival pigment
on paper, mounted
on panel, 25" x 35"

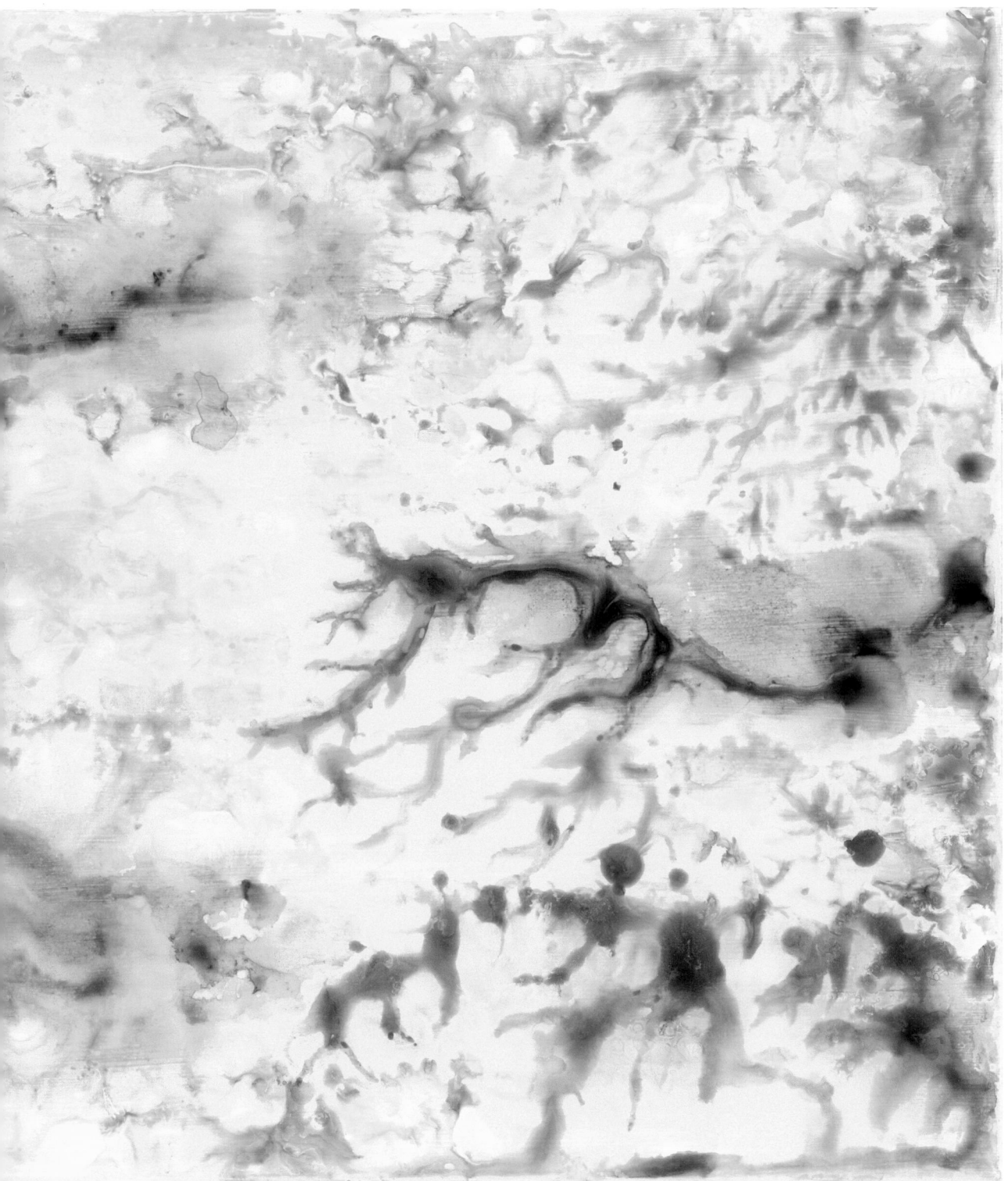

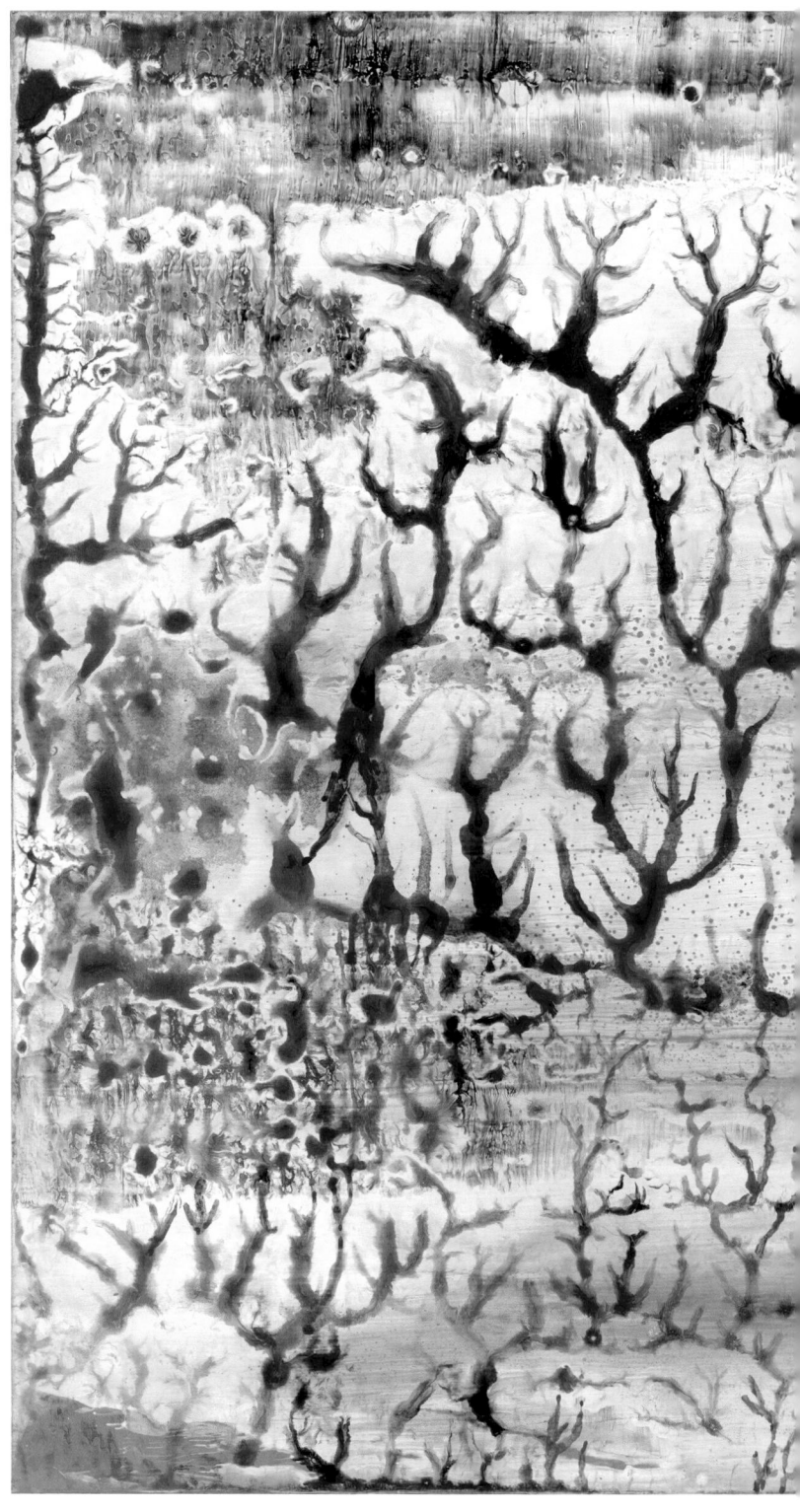

*Winter (1)*
2014
Archival pigment
on paper, mounted
on panel, 30" x 45"

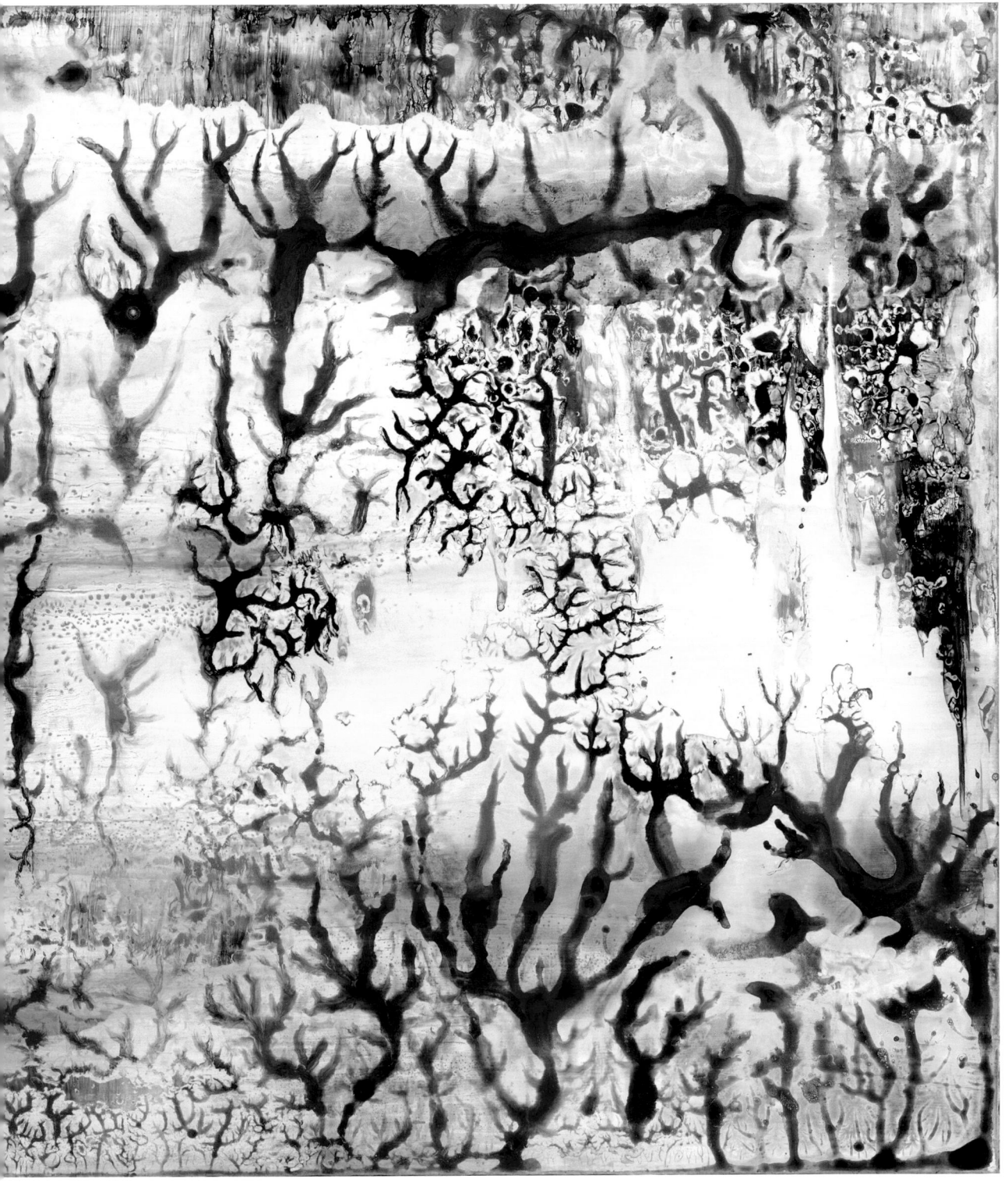

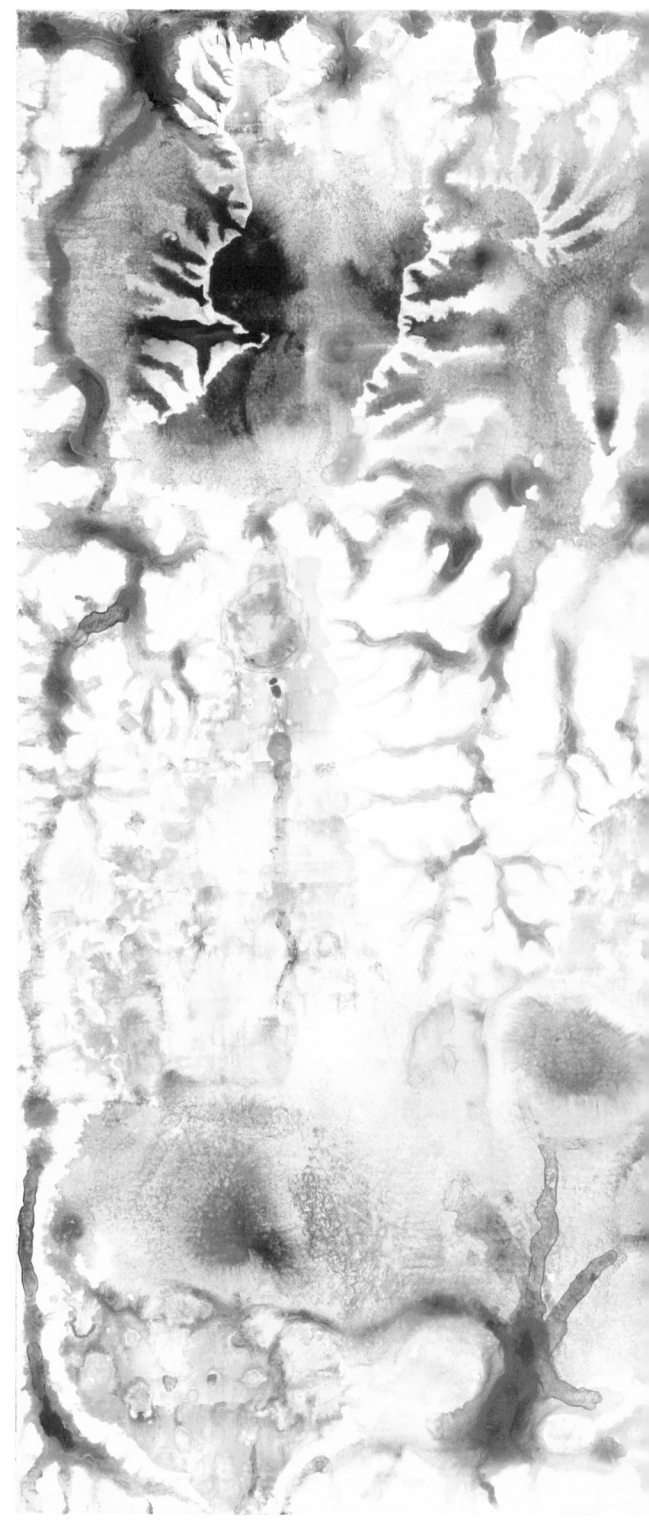

*Spring (1)*
2014
Archival pigment
on paper, mounted
on panel, 25" x 35"

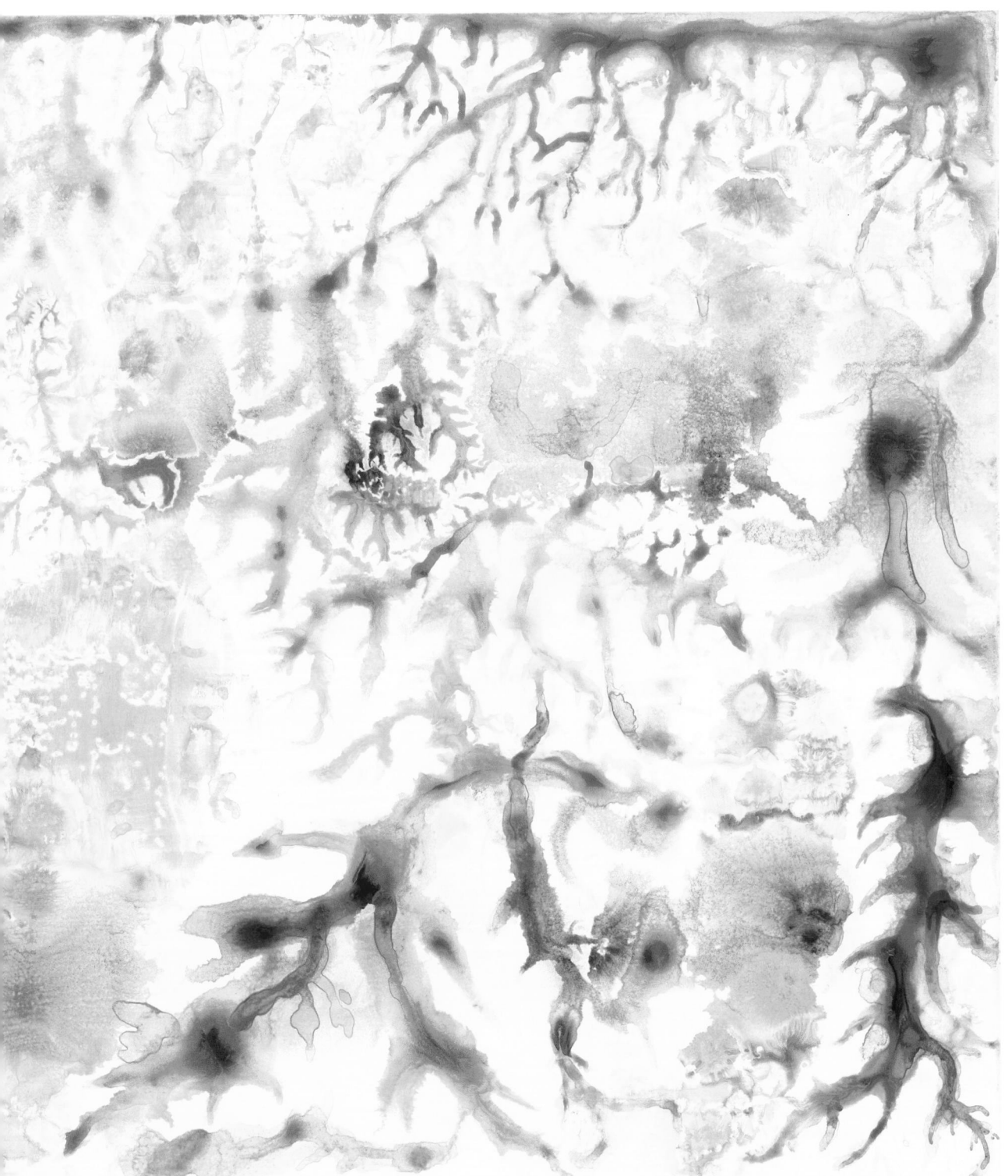

*Pond*
2014
Archival pigment
on paper, mounted
on panel, 48" x 36"

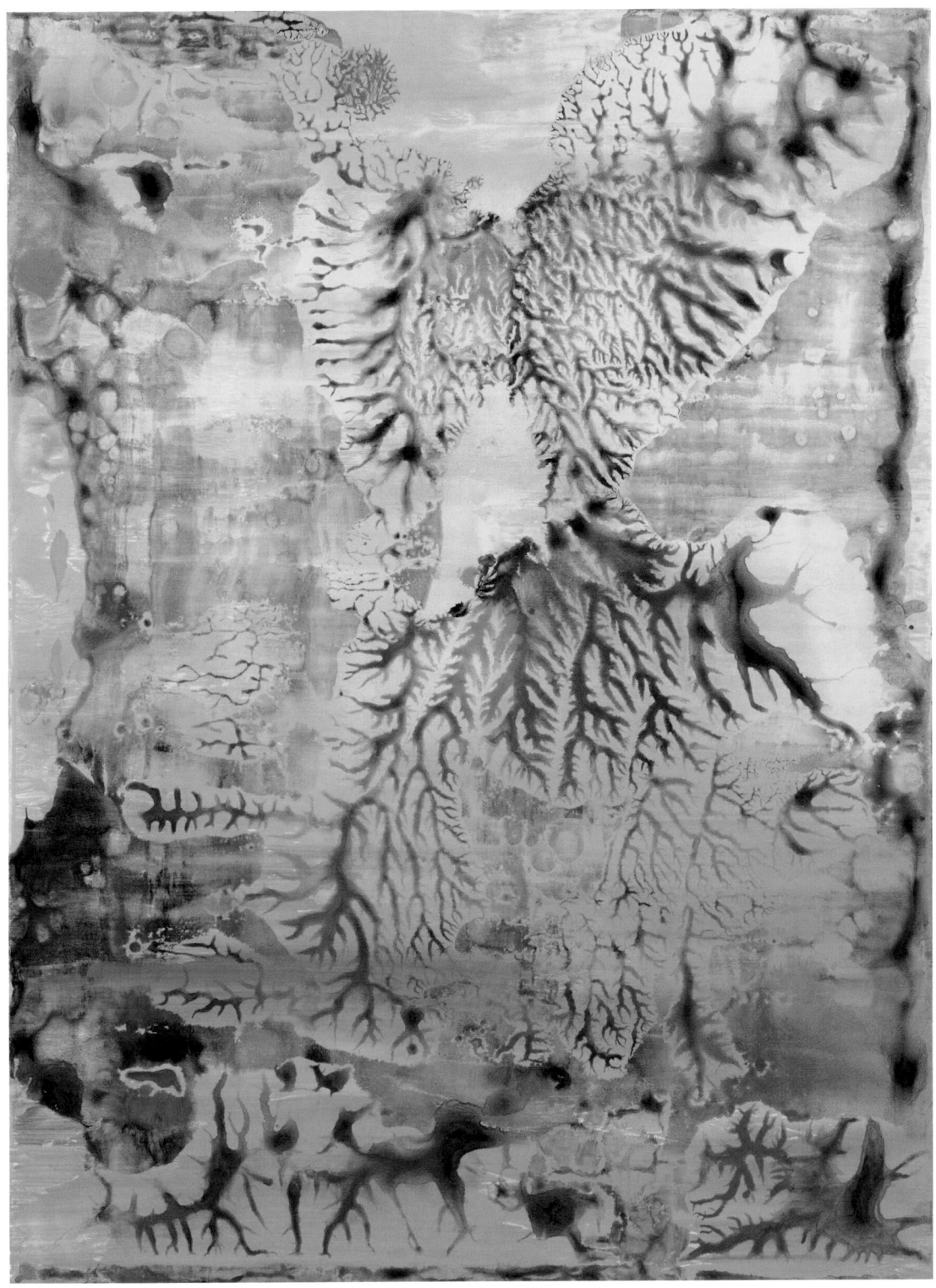

**Pond (2)**
2014
Archival pigment
on paper, mounted
on panel, 35" x 25"

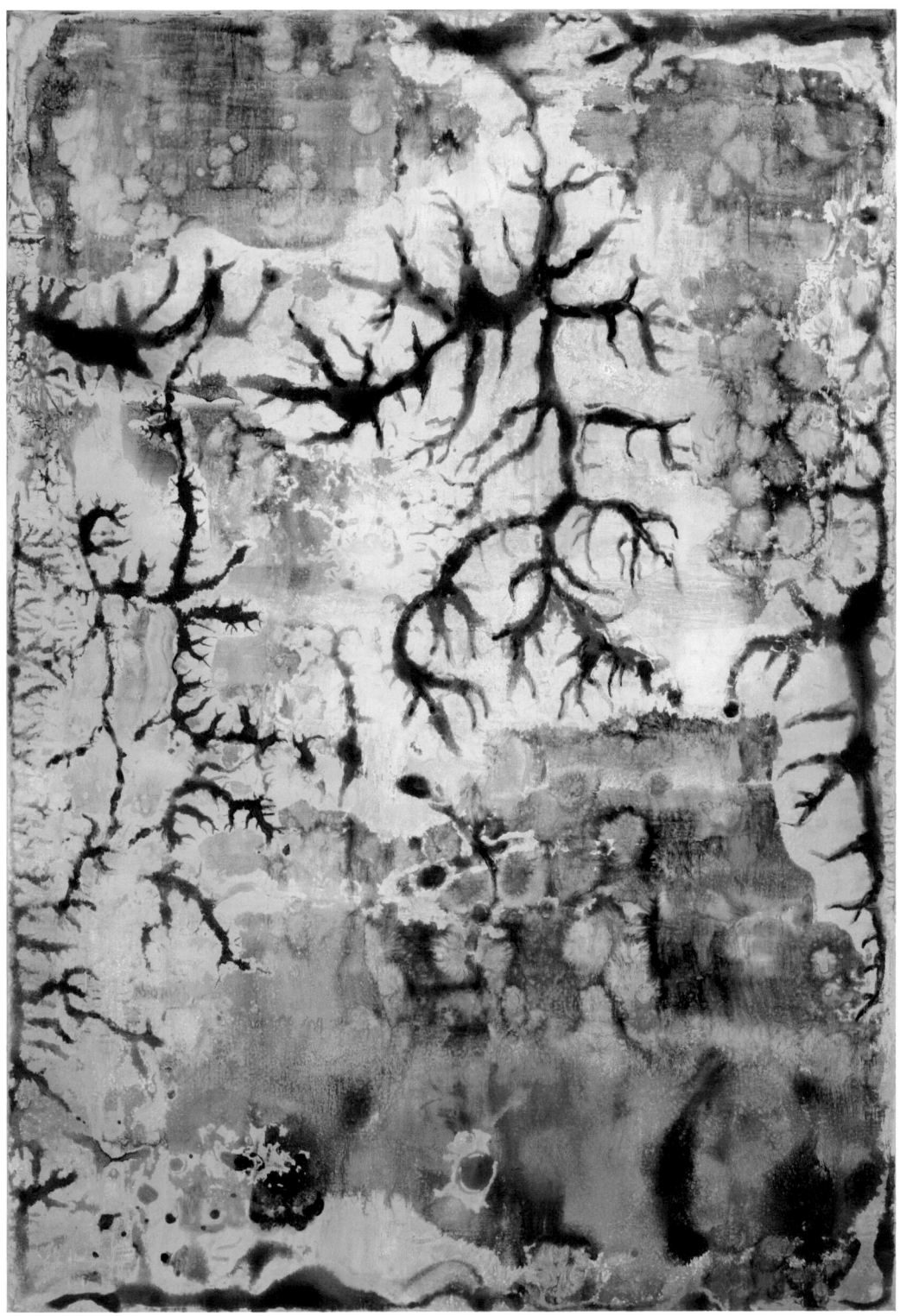

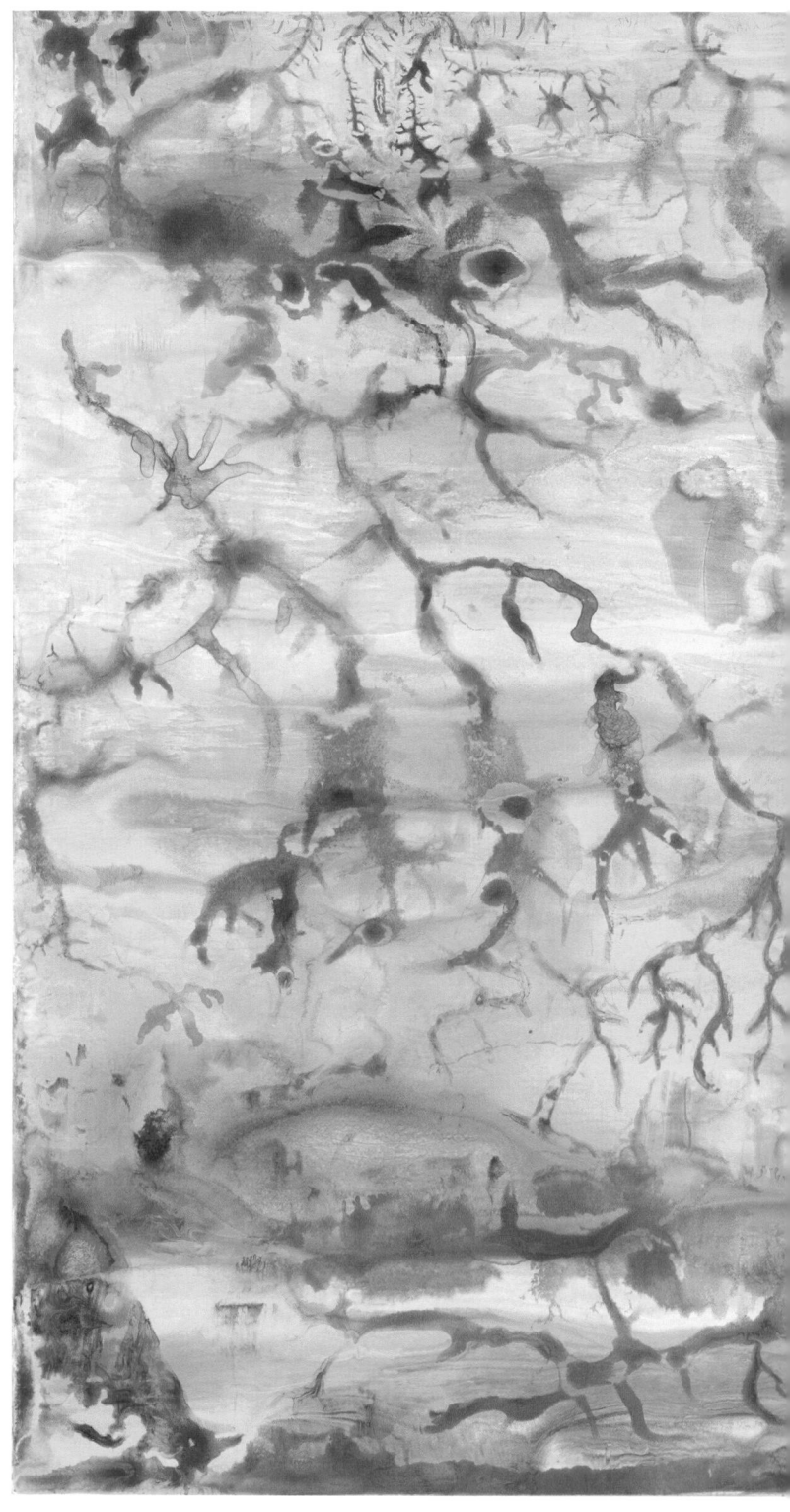

*Summer (1)*
2014
Archival pigment
on paper, mounted
on panel, 15" x 22"

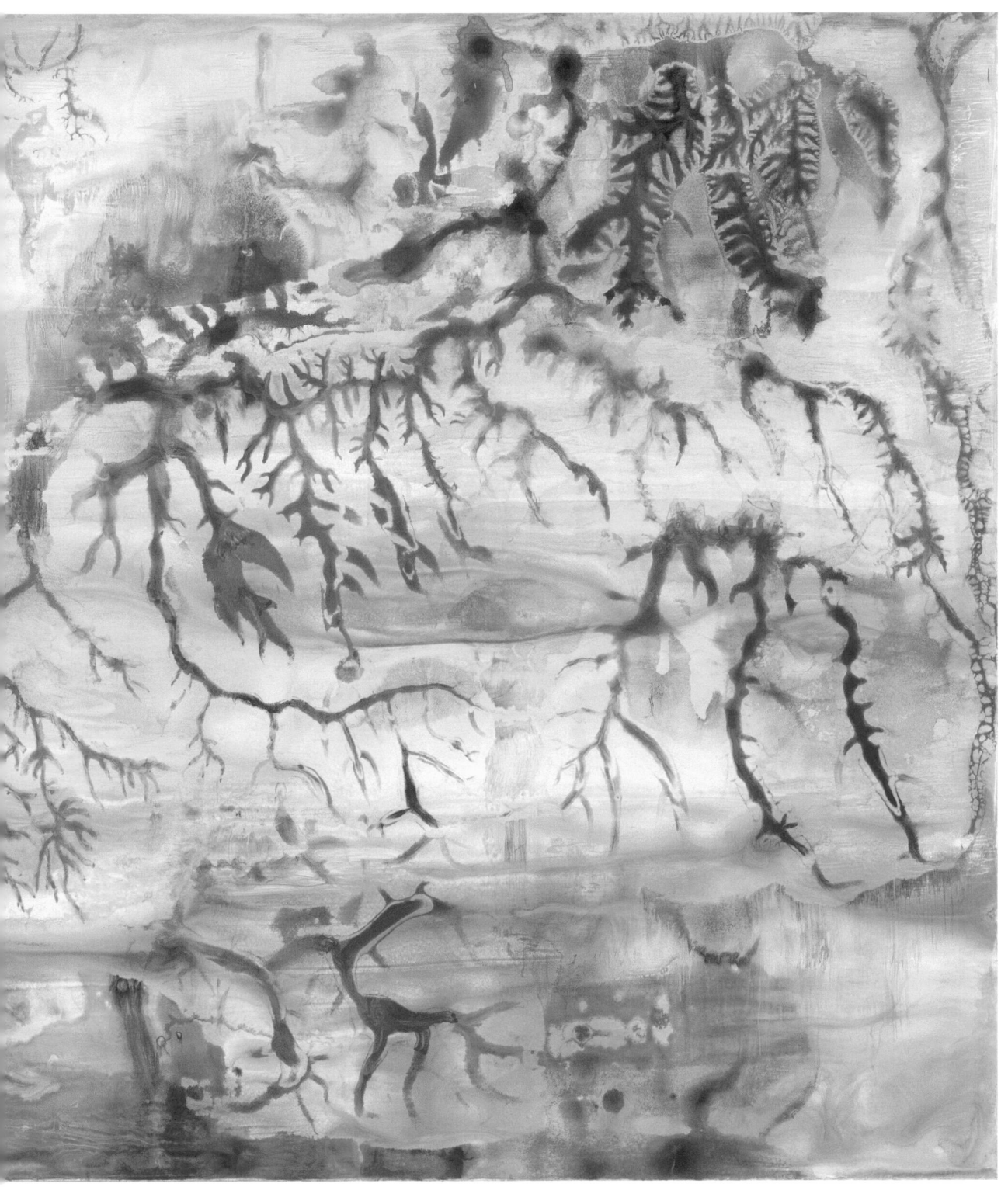

*Ground Fog*
2014
Archival pigment
on paper, mounted
on panel, 48" x 36"

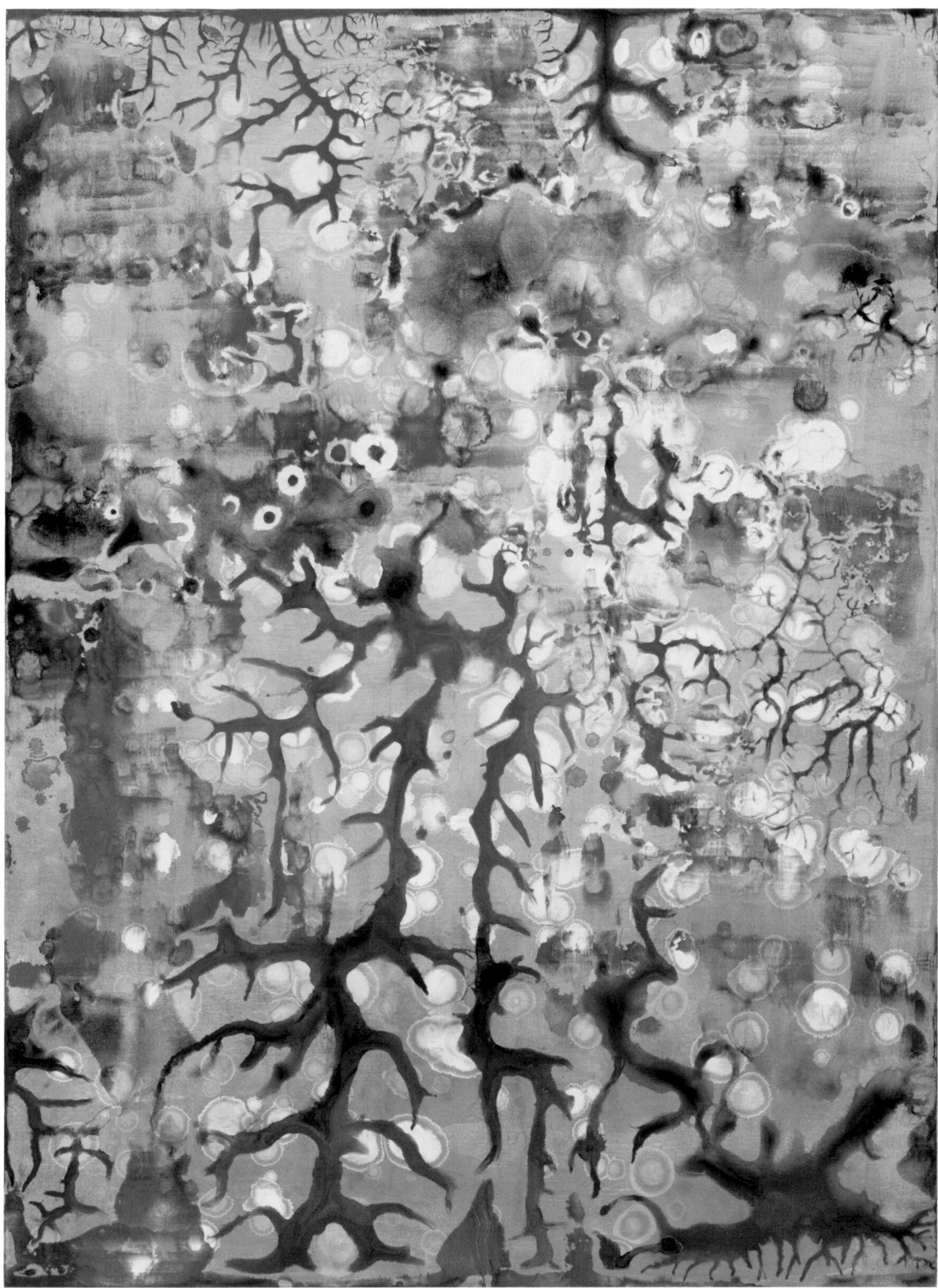

*Mountain*
2014
Archival pigment
on paper, mounted
on panel, 72" x 36"

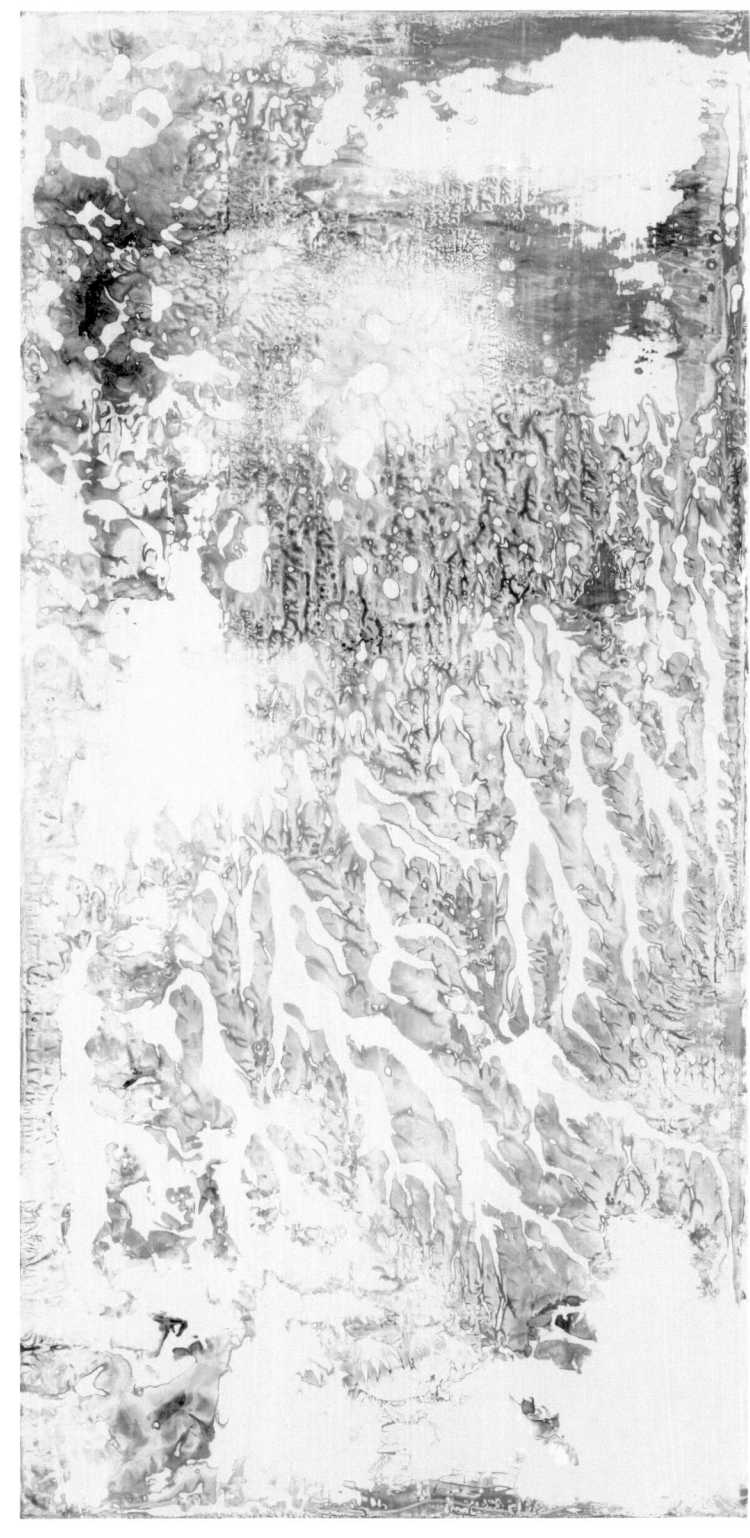

*White Light*
2014
Archival pigment
on paper, mounted
on panel, 40" x 30"

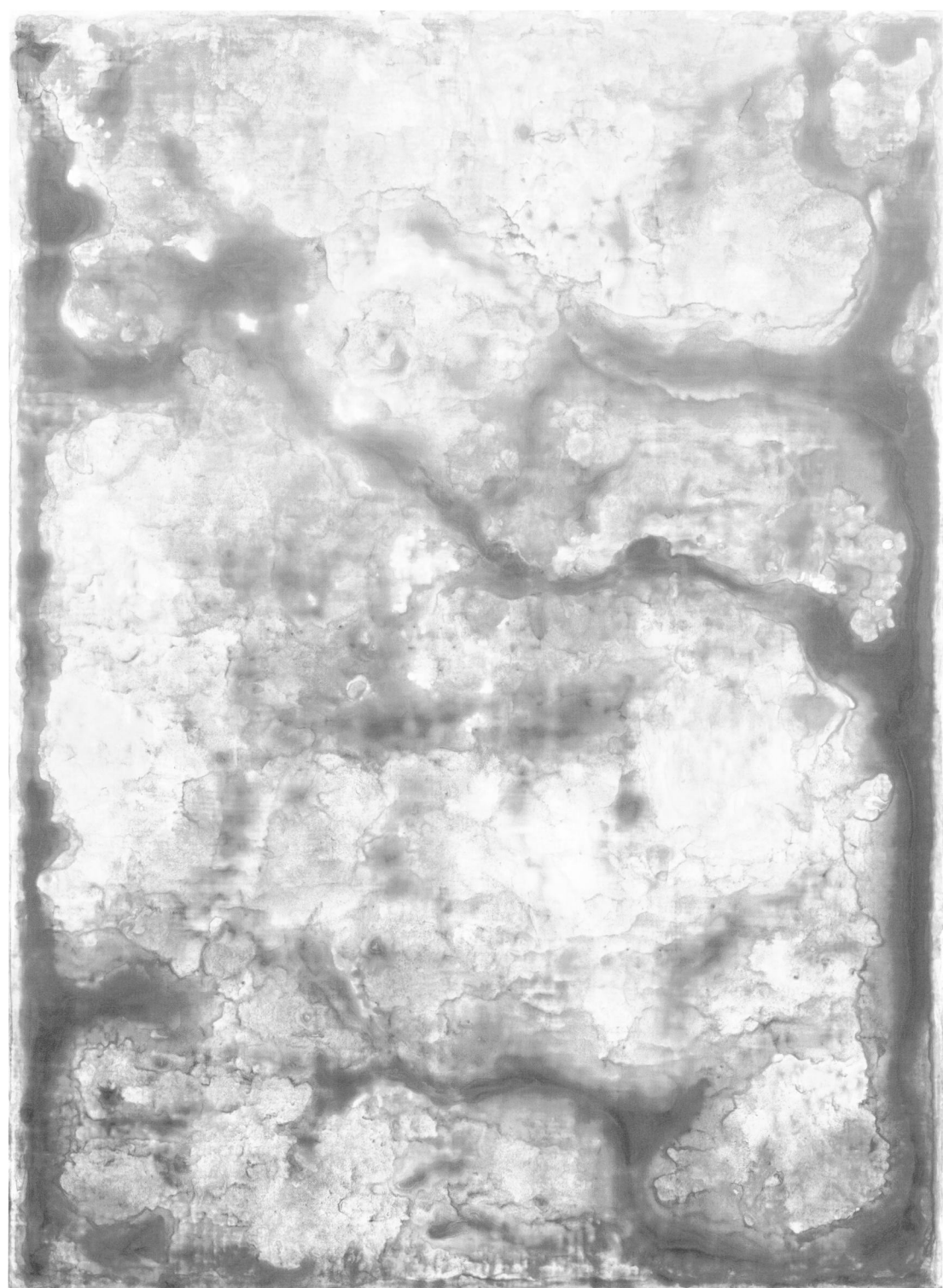

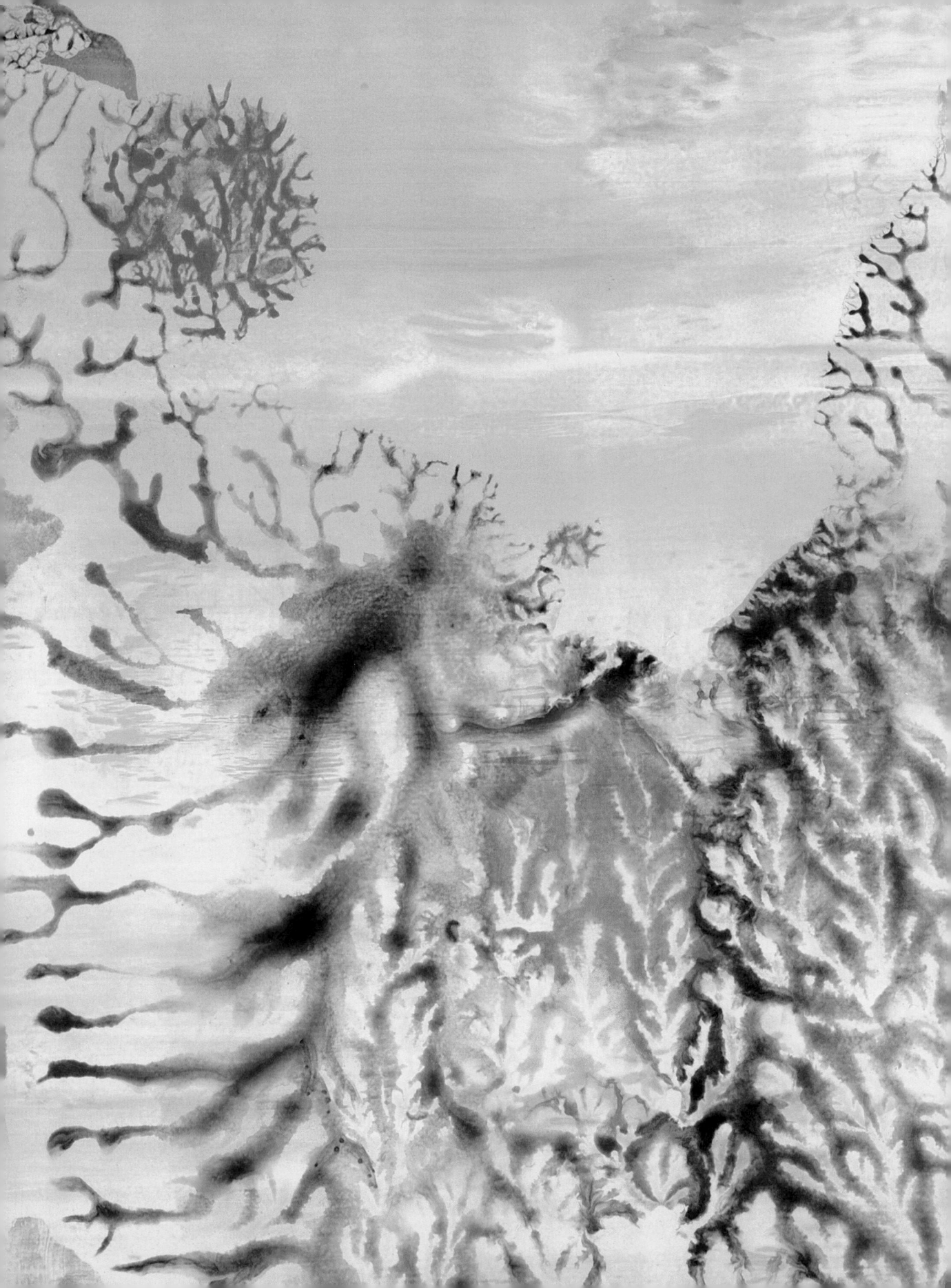

# Clearings: The Inner Landscapes of Karen Barth
Michael Steger

The fact that she gave her paintings titles that suggest landscapes—*Mountain, Pond, Winter*—does not preclude the possibility that Barth was inspired by images of nature that could just as easily be microscopic or from an aerial or satellite camera.

*Halfglimpses of the sea*
*Waterfalls*
*Shockheaded trees dripping moss*
*Heavy leaves rubbery shiny*
*Varnished with sun*
*A finely polished heat*
*Glitter*
*I'm not listening anymore to the animated conversations*
*of my friends who are mulling over*
*among themselves all the gossip I brought from Paris*
*On both sides of the train over our heads or else on the slope*
*of a distant valley opposite*
*The forest is there staring me down disturbing me attracts my eye*
*like the blank maskstare of a mummy*
*I stare back*
*No trace of an eye*

—Blaise Cendrars, "Clearings"
(translated from the French by John Dos Passos)[1]

I do not know what Karen Barth thought of the poetry of Cendrars, but this poem strikes me as an apt point of departure for discussing her last paintings. Blaise Cendrars wrote "Clearings" in the early 1920s, inspired by a train journey he made in Brazil. In the poem, the poet travels through landscapes that are utterly alien to him. These landscapes, seen through the windows of his train, seduce him away from the people conversing around him, drawing his gaze outside into foreign expanses that are simultaneously enchanting and unsettling.

Barth's last paintings, like Cendrars' poem, offer up strange and seductive vistas. For many of the poets and painters

*Pond* (detail)
2014
Archival pigment on paper, mounted on panel, 48" x 36"

associated with Surrealism, from René Char to Max Ernst, landscape represented mystery, a counterpoint to the rules and regulations of civilization. For the Surrealists, creating fantastic landscapes was a way of escaping what André Breton called "the reign of logic" and "absolute rationalism."[2] "Poetry" he wrote, "is made in the forest."[3]

Freud also used the analogy of looking at landscapes through a train window to describe the psychoanalytic technique of free association.[4] The projection of unconscious visions and desires does not end with the creation of the poem or painting. The work created—if it is vital enough, compelling enough, as in Barth's last paintings—becomes itself a screen onto which subsequent viewers project their own readings, and misreadings, and in so doing inevitably draw on their own conscious intents, their wishes and fears, their personal experience, and the sedimented layers of collective cultural memory.

Barth once wrote that she began her work with "photographs of the natural world." She did not elaborate as to the specific subjects of these photographs, and the fact that she gave her paintings titles that suggest landscapes—*Mountain*, *Pond*, *Winter*—does not preclude the possibility that Barth was inspired by images of nature that could just as easily be microscopic or from an aerial or satellite camera. "The photographic image," Barth once said, "stops the chatter and churn of my mind and places me in the present moment. The painting begins." Walking into a gallery space filled with Barth's last works, made in 2014, I feel as though I am traveling on the train of Cendrars and Freud. I think again of the poet, absorbed by the world outside his window, turning away from the chatter of his friends on the train. Barth's statement makes it clear that the act of painting is, for her, synonymous with "the present moment." And yet the present isn't an isolated cell of time. It is, rather, a crystallization of time, an intersection of our personal histories with much broader cultural and social histories. As we look at Barth's paintings, we too "stop the chatter" around us and engage with each painting in the present.

One naturally views the four large paintings named for the four seasons as imaginary landscapes that—as in the

"The photographic image," Barth once said, "stops the chatter and churn of my mind and places me in the present moment. The painting begins."

*Fall* (detail)
2014
Archival pigment
on paper, mounted
on panel, 40" x 80"

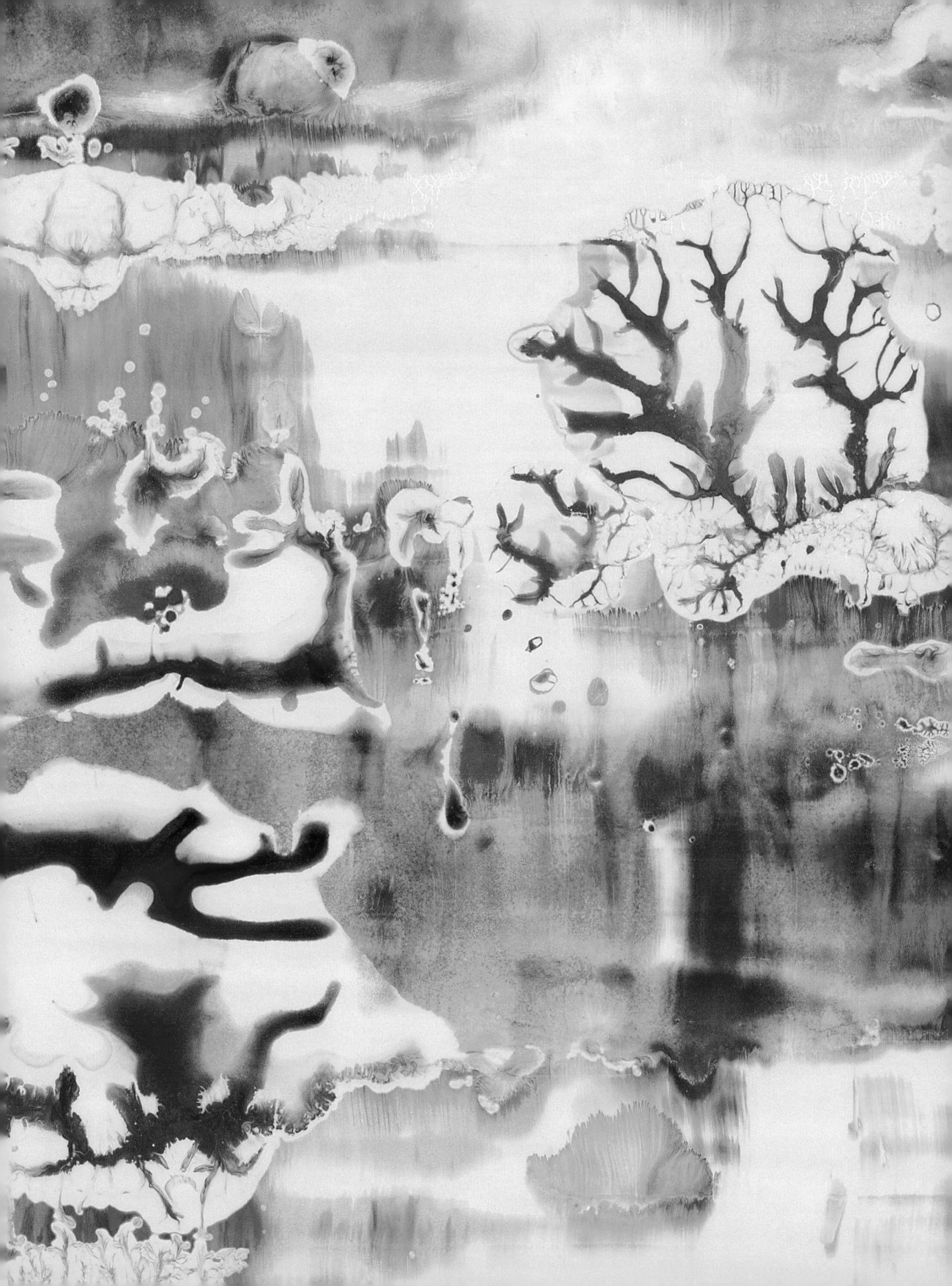

Cendrars poem—simultaneously seduce and repel. The colors of the paintings range from the nearly monochromatic *White Light* to the almost sickly-sweet combinations of acid pinks and greens in *Spring (I)*. A feast of exploding greens in *Spring* is interspersed with rose and unsaturated violets in a deep, atmospheric space glimpsed through the rhizome-stain network which here resembles nothing so much as a dense cluster of thorns.

In *Summer* there are bigger gaps (clearings) among the rhizome-stain networks through which we perceive, just to the left of center and in several other places, attenuating horizontal light and dark bands that suggest ripples on water. Here, as if in counterpoint to the upward-thrusting movement of *Spring*, the root-like networks hang down. Around the edges of the painting are green stains reminiscent of algae or mold. Indeed, I can dimly imagine in *Summer* what might be a large photograph of a sea-coast in the process of being covered by some fungal growth. An imaginative viewer might even be inclined to see a form as a green sailing ship or an underwater tableau.

*Fall* shifts into a palette of earthy red and orange hues. The rhizome-stain forms have moved mainly to the right and left sides, coming together across the top of the painting. The fragmented root forms in the upper center suggest the rack of a stag displayed starkly in a hunting lodge. Fall is, after all, the season of the hunt. The open expanses of this painting remind me of the paradigmatic *Waste Land* of T. S. Eliot:

> "A heap of broken images,
>  where the sun beats,
>  And the dead tree gives no shelter,
>  the cricket no relief,
>  And the dry stone no sound of water."

In contrast to the desolation of *Fall*, *Winter* comes as something of a relief, with its cool blues and deep greens. There is the hint of a horizon on the right, as if one were looking across a bay or inlet, above which is a patch of what resembles blue sky. Here the dark, upward-reaching root forms take on a figural quality within the prevalence of white and light blues, remind me of the dark figures in one of the best-known paintings of winter, Bruegel's *Hunters in the Snow* of 1565.

As if through a door or over a threshold, Barth's vertical paintings create a sense of atmospheric space which draws us in. *Pond* seems to take us down beneath the water. I think here of the Shakespearean title of Pollock's 1947 vertical painting, *Full Fathom Five*. Whereas Pollock's painting records a male artist's legendary physical struggle with the canvas, in which his physical presence—not to mention the detritus of his studio—is everywhere asserted, in front of *Pond* we may not even feel certain we are looking at the results of deliberate, conscious human making. Rather, *Pond*—like all of Barth's last paintings—appears to be the product of chance operations, or some organic, self-perpetuating process, like the spread of a stain or the chain of a chemical reaction.

The longer we regard *Pond*, the more we begin to notice the formal decisions Barth made. We see, for instance, sections where the rhizome-stains are set against the edges of a lighter area of color. These edges become most apparent against another, darker area that appears to be behind the lighter color. For example, if we focus on the two large rhizome-stains that dominate the upper central area of the painting, or the long, attenuated section that runs along the left edge and across the bottom, the figure-ground relationships we might have perceived previously are called into question: Are the blue-grey areas that envelope nearly all of the root-forms a background, or do they constitute a figure, standing out against a background? Discerning these ambiguous spatial relationships, one cannot help but feel how Barth understood that when traveling in, or passing through, actual physical landscapes, this confusion occurs often: Is that stand of trees within walking distance? Is that range of hills receding or am I getting closer to it?

In *Ground Fog*—with its palette of violets and its orbs of light—the illusion of depth is almost vertiginous: Are the rhizomatic forms figures, or are they fissures in the pale violet clouds that permeate the painting? Are those green stains on the surface, or are they floating in the distance?

I turn now to one last painting, *Mountain*, a wintery, vertical landscape. *Mountain* is one of the only works in which the rhizome structures are rendered in whites, though behind these pale root-like structures we glimpse the dark forms that we have seen in other paintings from this final period. This painting evokes for me another famous winter scene, a triptych of woodcut prints, *Kiso Mountains in Snow* by Hiroshige, from 1857, in the collection of the Metropolitan Museum. It is a testimony to the power and reach of Barth's last paintings that they resonate with the work of Hiroshige and Bruegel no less than with modern and postmodern Western painting.

Modernism has nearly always been characterized by a clear manifestation of form and structure. Surveying Karen Barth's last paintings, it is impossible to ignore the way they undermine this formal language, i.e. the visual vocabulary of straight lines, grids, monochrome fields. Barth's last works clearly call this formal assertion into question in much the same way that Cendrars, in his poem, calls into question what it is that should claim the focus of our vision and our thoughts. Barth's paintings, like Cendrars's poem, open up clearings in the mind. Returning to the rich heritage of Surrealism, they might be viewed in relation to Georges Bataille's influential definition of "the *formless*." Bataille wrote, "[F]ormless is not only an adjective having a given meaning, but a term that serves to bring things down into the world, generally requiring that each thing have its form. What it designates has no rights in any sense and gets itself squashed everywhere, like a spider or an earthworm. In fact, for academic men to be happy, the universe would have to take shape. [. . .] On the other hand, affirming that the universe resembles nothing and is only *formless* amounts to saying that the universe is something like a spider or spit."[5]

We might well see Barth's late paintings as being, among many other things, an act of resistance against "academic men." (Barth was, at other points in her career, a more overtly feminist artist.) In opposition to the academicisms of both modernism and postmodernism, Barth's last paintings are the product of a female visual artist working—no less than did John Cage in the realm of sound—with randomized operations and allusions to unconscious

*Mountain* (detail)
2014
Archival pigment
on paper, mounted
on panel, 72" x 36"

processes and the natural, disordered environment. These paintings tap into deep and primitive—and indeed formless—feelings about what it is like to exist, as we inevitably do, in a fractal, dissolving, decaying landscape, whether that landscape be on a microscopic, human, or astronomical scale.

Karen Barth's last paintings are also full of ironies—not least of which is the fact that they are not paintings properly speaking, but very high quality digital productions based on small-scale paintings made by the artist's hand. This would take us solidly into the realm of questions posed by Walter Benjamin in his seminal 1936 essay, "The Work of Art in the Age of Mechanical Reproduction." I have, however, chosen not to focus on this ironic aspect of the last paintings but on what I see to be their lineage within three converging lines of thought: the modern lineage of Surrealism; the centuries-old lineage of landscape; and the deep lineage of human awareness that everything seems to dissolve and decay into, and also grow out of, everything else.

There are, undoubtedly, many ways of entering into and reading these paintings. It may well be that my thoughts here represent nothing but the free associations of one viewer who has succumbed with pleasure to the spell of Karen Barth's last paintings. In any case, it is, without question, a great tribute to Karen Barth that her final series of paintings carry with them the potential for a rich and varied range of powerful associations. Her last paintings are, indeed, a tribute to a very human imagination, culture, and to memory.

**Michael Steger** is an artist and writer who teaches color theory and painting at Hunter College. He lives and works in the Hudson Valley and Manhattan.

1
*Échappées sur la mer*
*Chutes d'eau*
*Arbres chevelus moussus*
*Lourdes feuilles caoutchoutées luisantes*
*Un vernis de soleil*
*Une chaleur bien astiquée*
*Reluisance*
*Je n'écoute plus la conversation animée de*
*mes amis qui se partagent les nouvelles que*
*j'ai apportees de Paris*
*Des deux côtés du train toute proche ou*
*alors de l'autre cote de la vallée lointaine*
*La forêt est là et me regarde et m'inquiète*
*et m'attire comme le masque d'une momie*
*Je regarde*
*Pas l'ombre d'une oeil*
"Trouées", Dos Passos translation from
*The Random House Book of Twentieth-*
*Century French Poetry*, Paul Auster, ed.,
New York: Random House, 1982,
pp. 105-106.

2
Breton, André. "First Manifesto of
Surrealism," in *Manifestoes of Surrealism*,
Seaver and Lane, transl., Ann Arbor:
University of Michigan Press, 1972, p. 9.

3
Breton, André. "Sur la route de San
Romano," (1941) from Auster, op cit., p. 194.

4
Freud, Sigmund. "On Beginning the
Treatment," (1913), Seulin, Christian,
transl., cited in *On Freud's "On Beginning
the Treatment,"* Seulin and Saragnano, eds.
London: Karnac Books, 2012, p. 135.

5
Bataille, Georges. *Visions of Excess:
Selected Writings*, 1927-1939. Alan Stoekel,
transl. Minneapolis: University of Minnesota
Press, 1985, p. 31.

Works 1992–2005

My work is involved with the question of what painting is, after Pollack, after Greenberg, after photography, in an increasingly digitalized age. Working with photographically derived landscape elements and a process that relies on both accident and intention, my objective is to reinvigorate the language of abstraction and the experience of landscape made remote by photography.

My paintings begin by selecting photographs of the natural world. The photographic image stops the chatter and churn of my mind and places me in the present moment. I employ a technique of pulling paint that simultaneously eradicates the classic gesture and creates unanticipated events. The act of pulling paint is also a response to photography and the way it smoothes out experience by rendering images on a flawless surface. I combine an illusion of chemical and/or technological alteration that has the quality of photographic emulsions and includes a vocabulary of painterly abstraction.

My method alternates between chaos, control, painterly and mechanical, to create a painting that is the result of a process, but also evokes elements of landscape. I use paint in a fluid way, to suggest water and its metaphorical associations to all that is mutable and unfixed. I look for an image that comprises the artificial and the natural, the abstract and the real, as well as a confluence between painting as process and nature as process. I endeavor to connect the viewer to the natural world via the phenomena of paint.

My work is a meditation on the complexity of my experience as altered by an increasingly technological environment. For me, a painting is complete when it suggests a kind of mystery that exists in a realm between sensation and thought.

Karen Barth

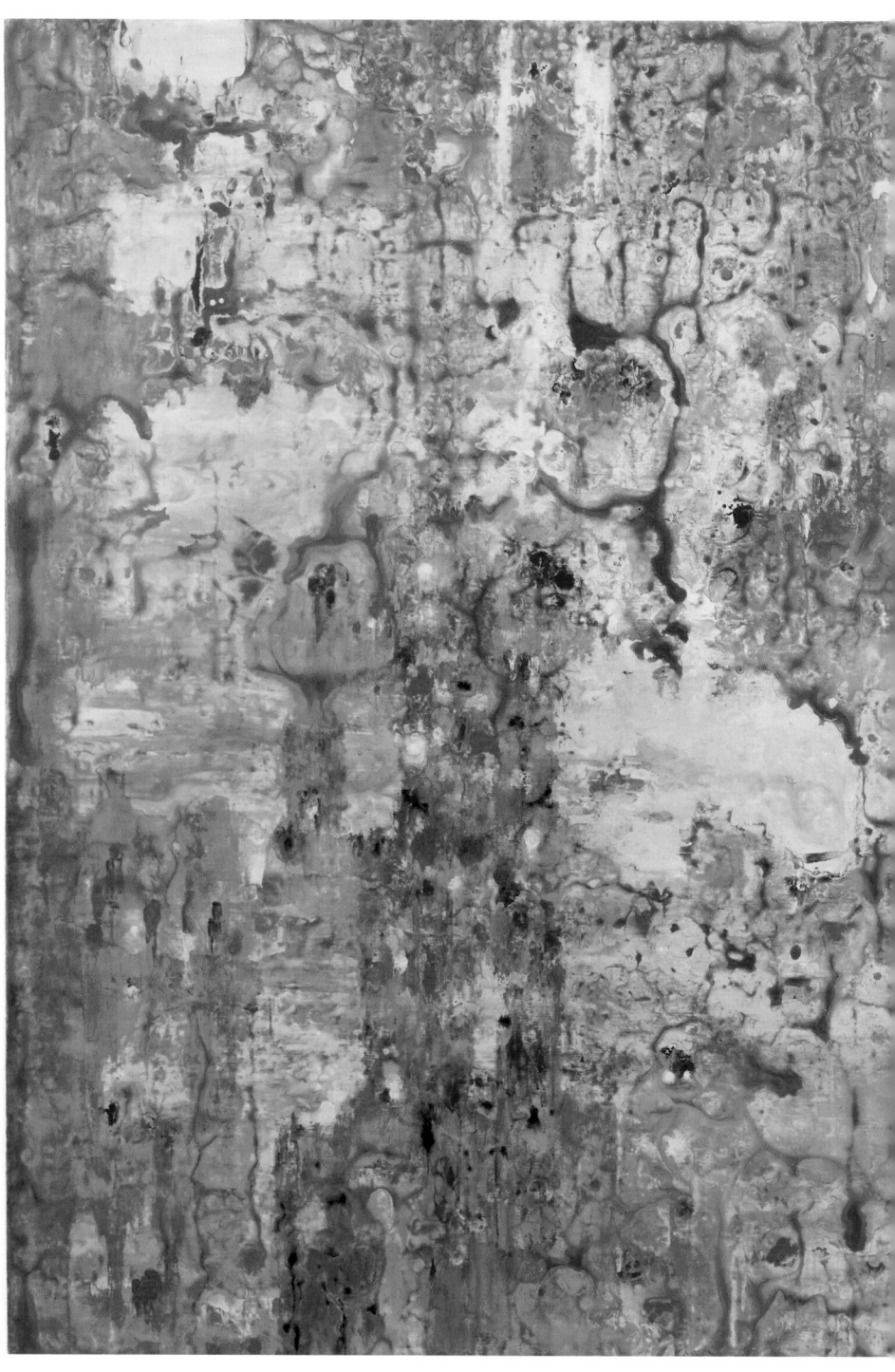

*Between Sensation &*
*Thought #12*
2005
Polymer on wood,
48" x 82"

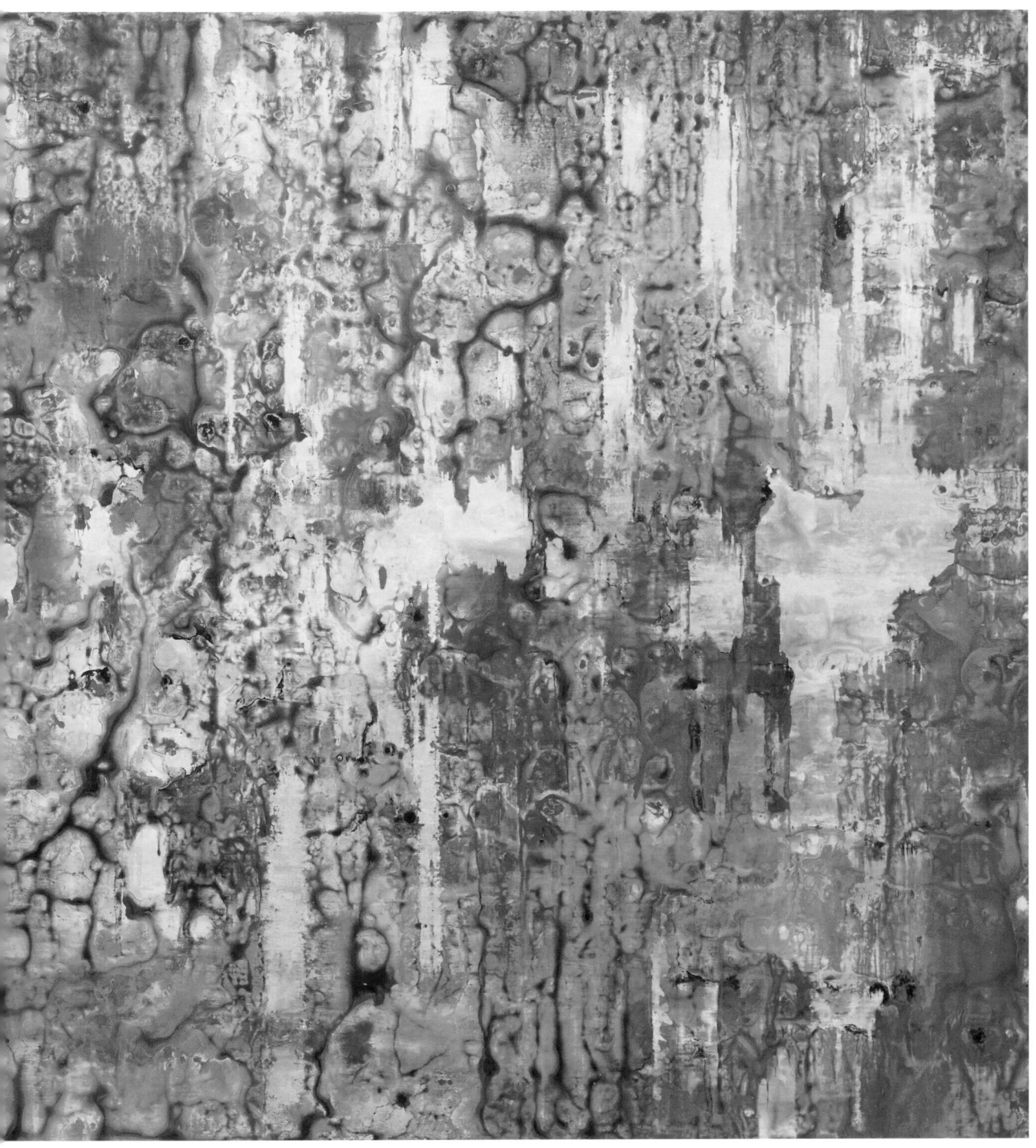

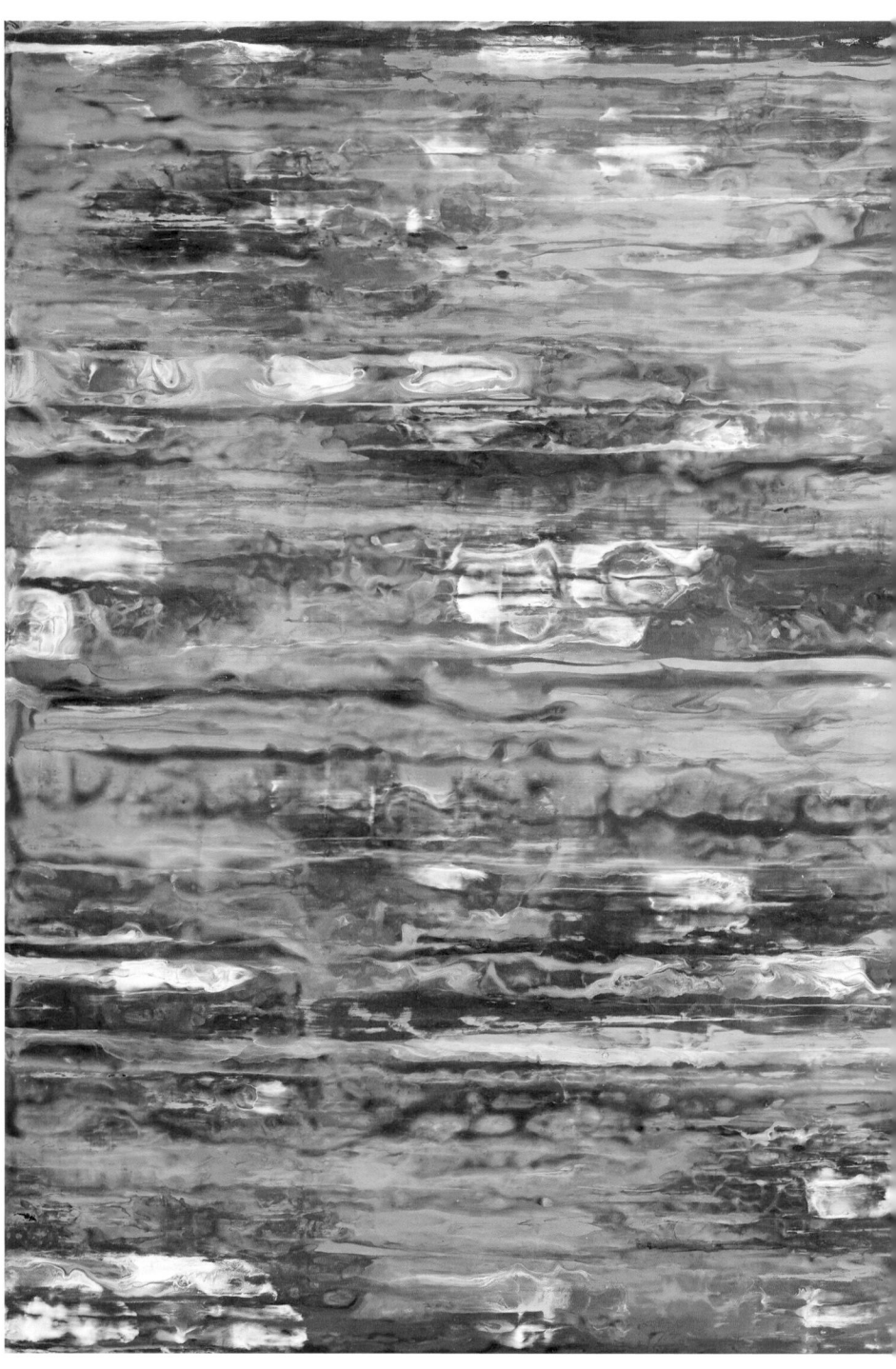

*Between Sensation &*
*Thought #13*
2005
Polymer on wood,
18" x 31"

**M.A.P.P. #4**
2001
Polymer on wood,
51" x 42"

**M.A.P.P. #5**
2001
Polymer on canvas
stretched over wood,
48" x 82"

*M.A.P.P. #1b*
2000
Polymer on wood,
16" x 20"

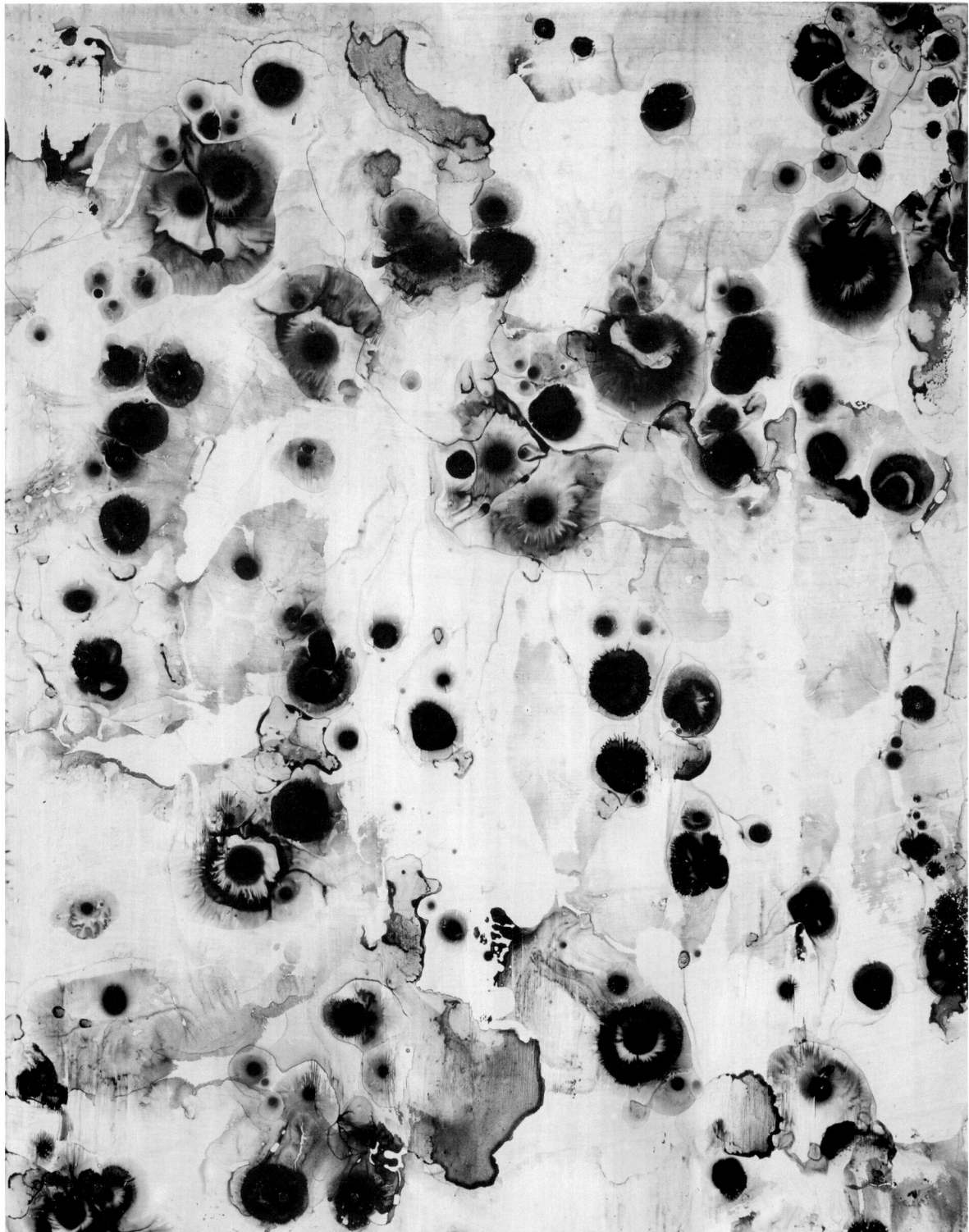

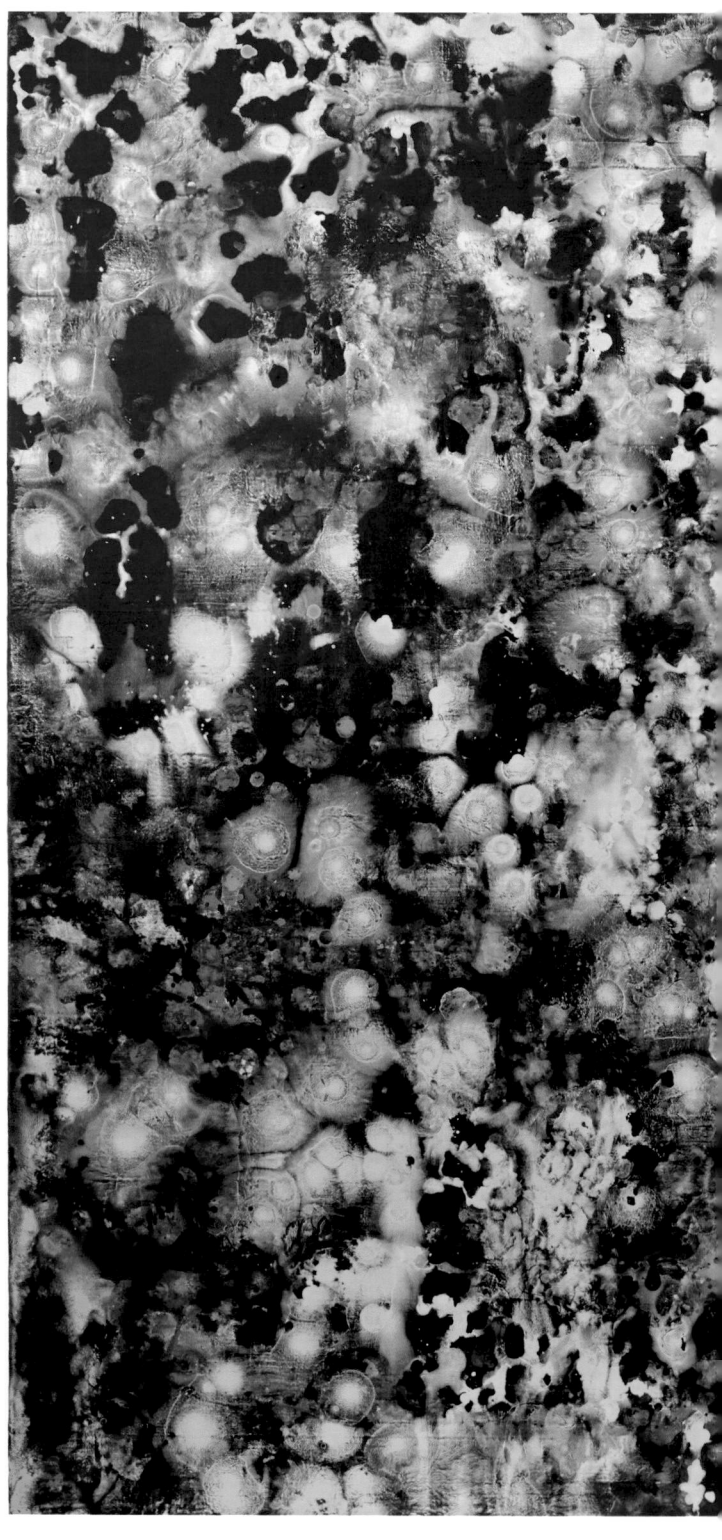

*M.A.P.P. #3*
2000
Polymer on canvas
stretched over wood,
56" x 82"

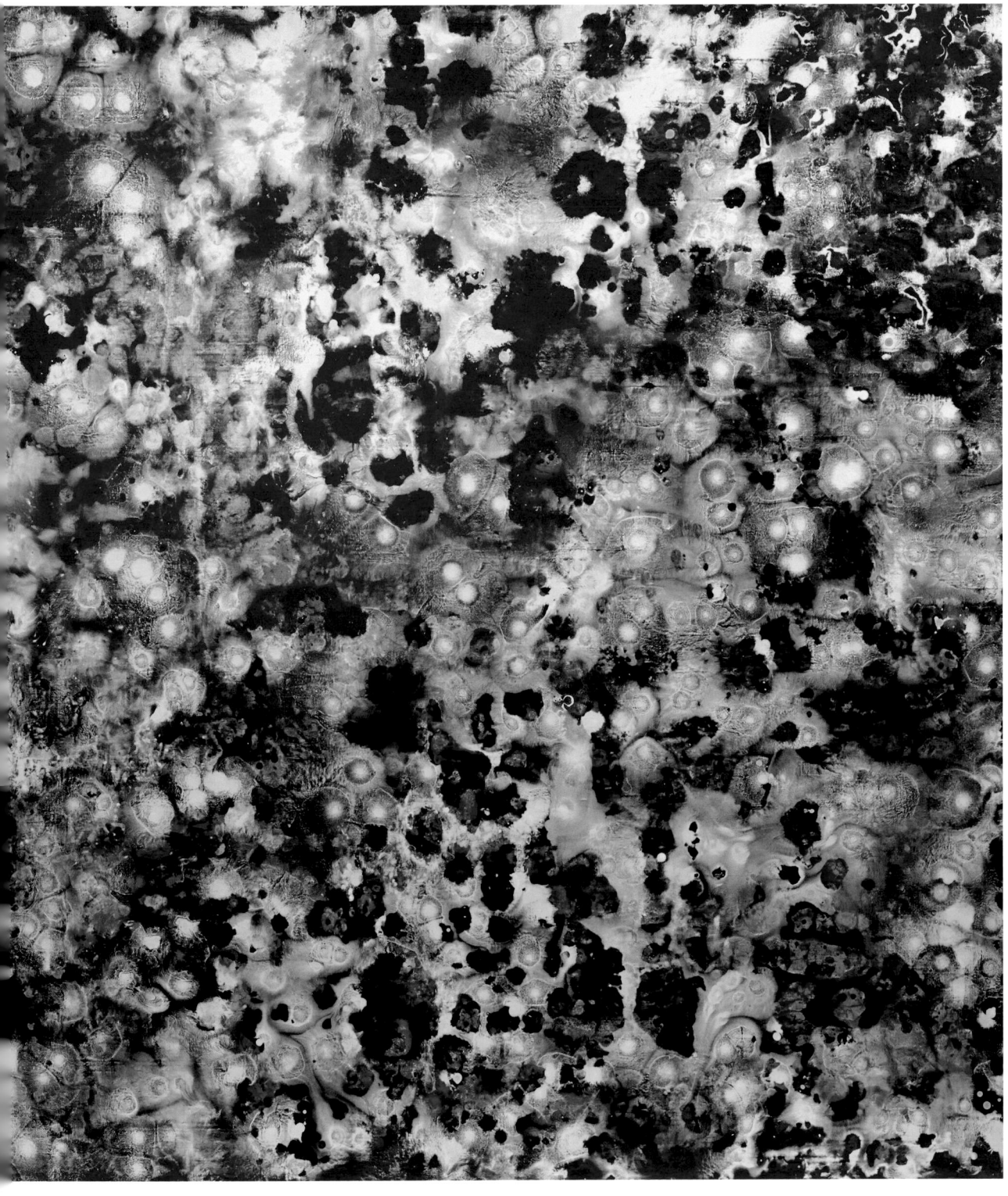

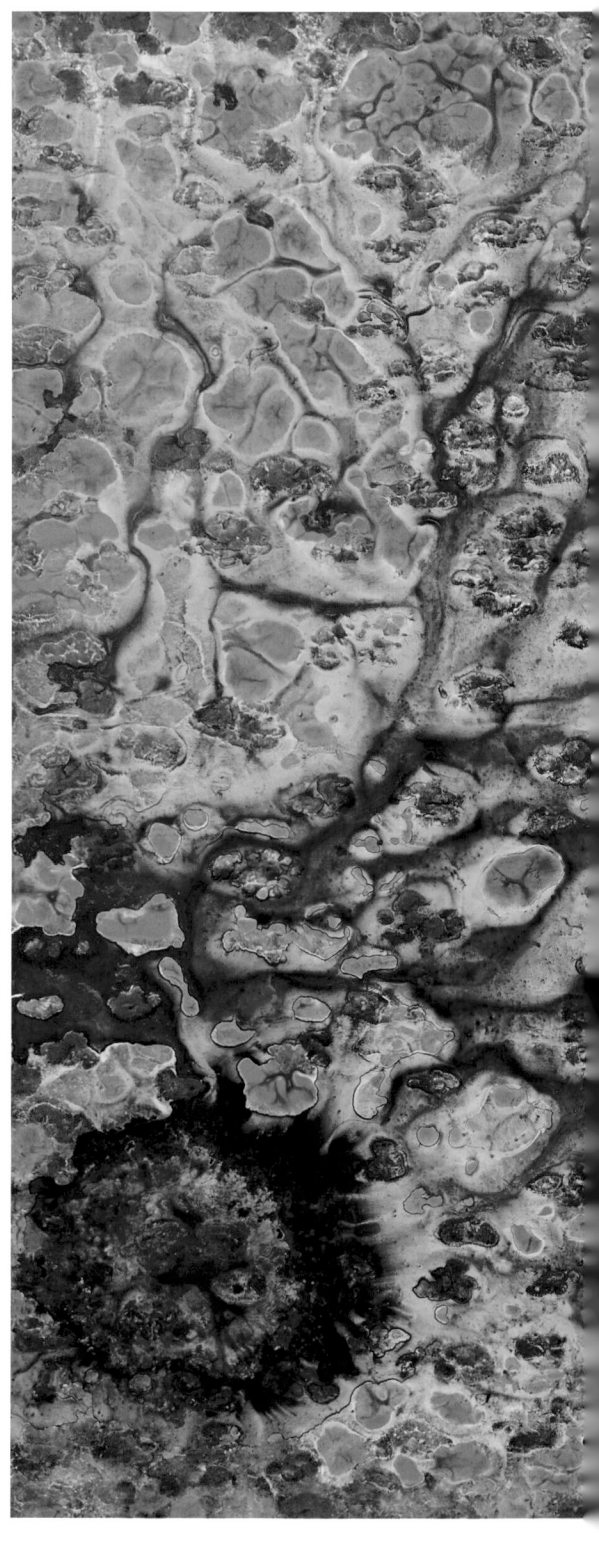

*Lake of Dreams II*
1995
Polymer on canvas
stretched on panel,
60" x 82"

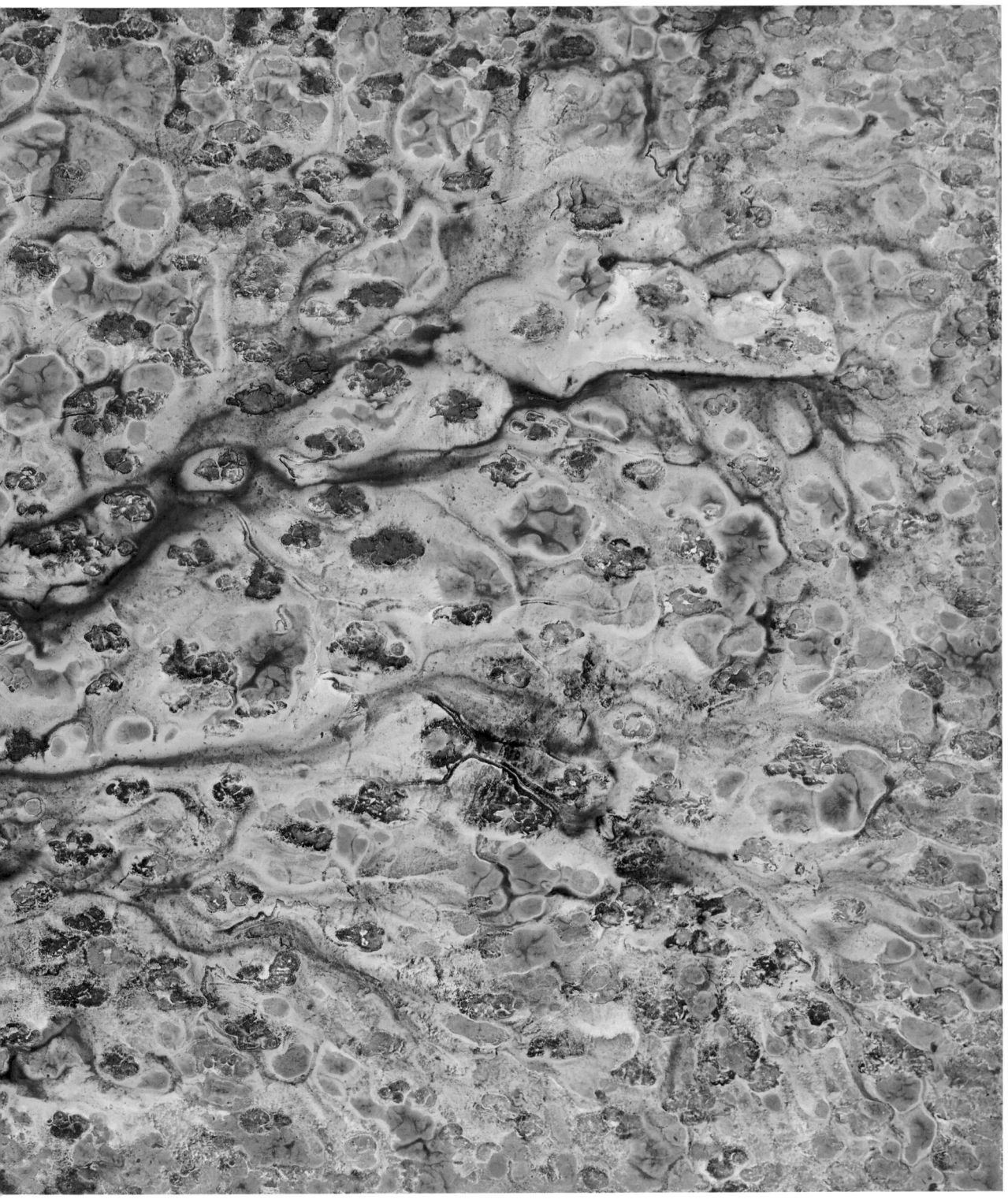

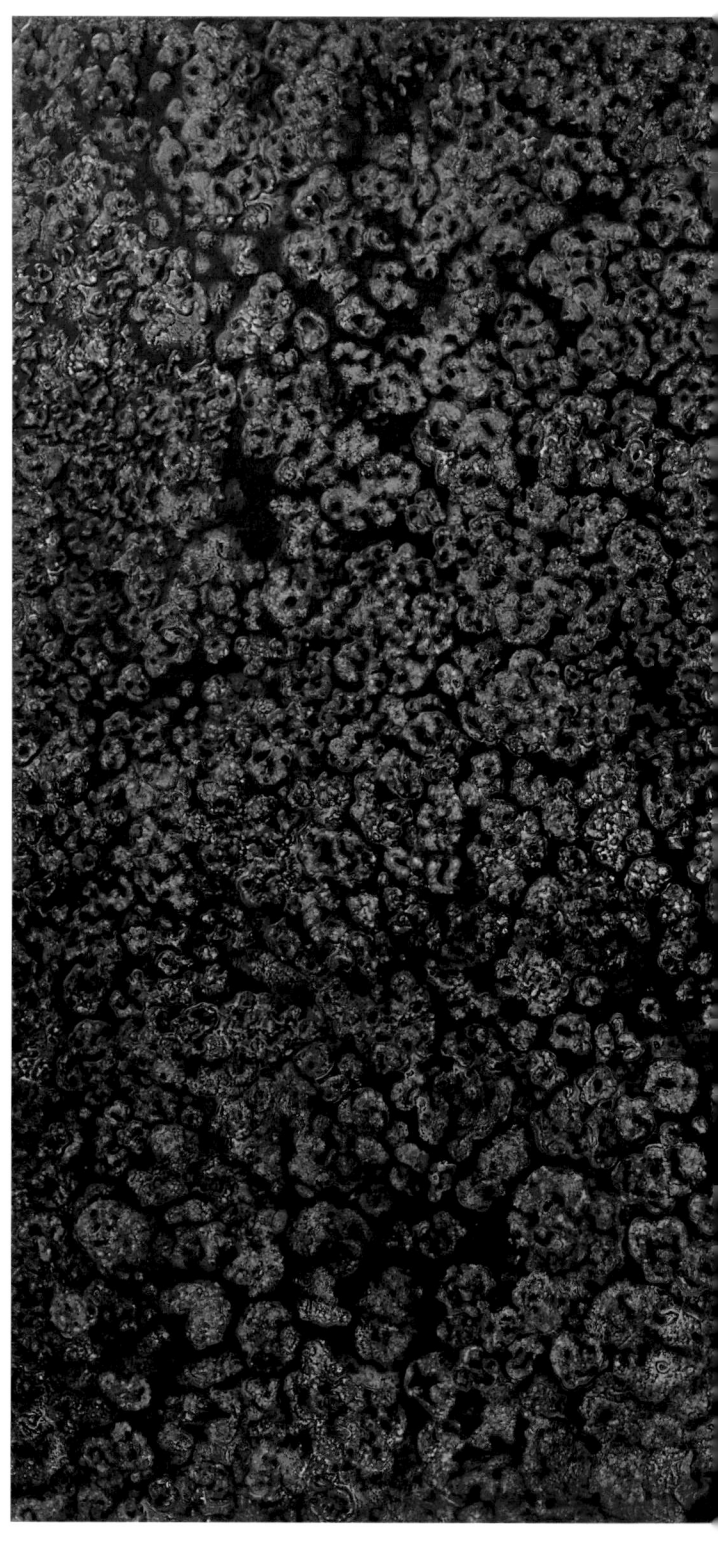

*Mind + Matter*
1992
Acrylic on canvas
stretched on panel,
56" x 82"

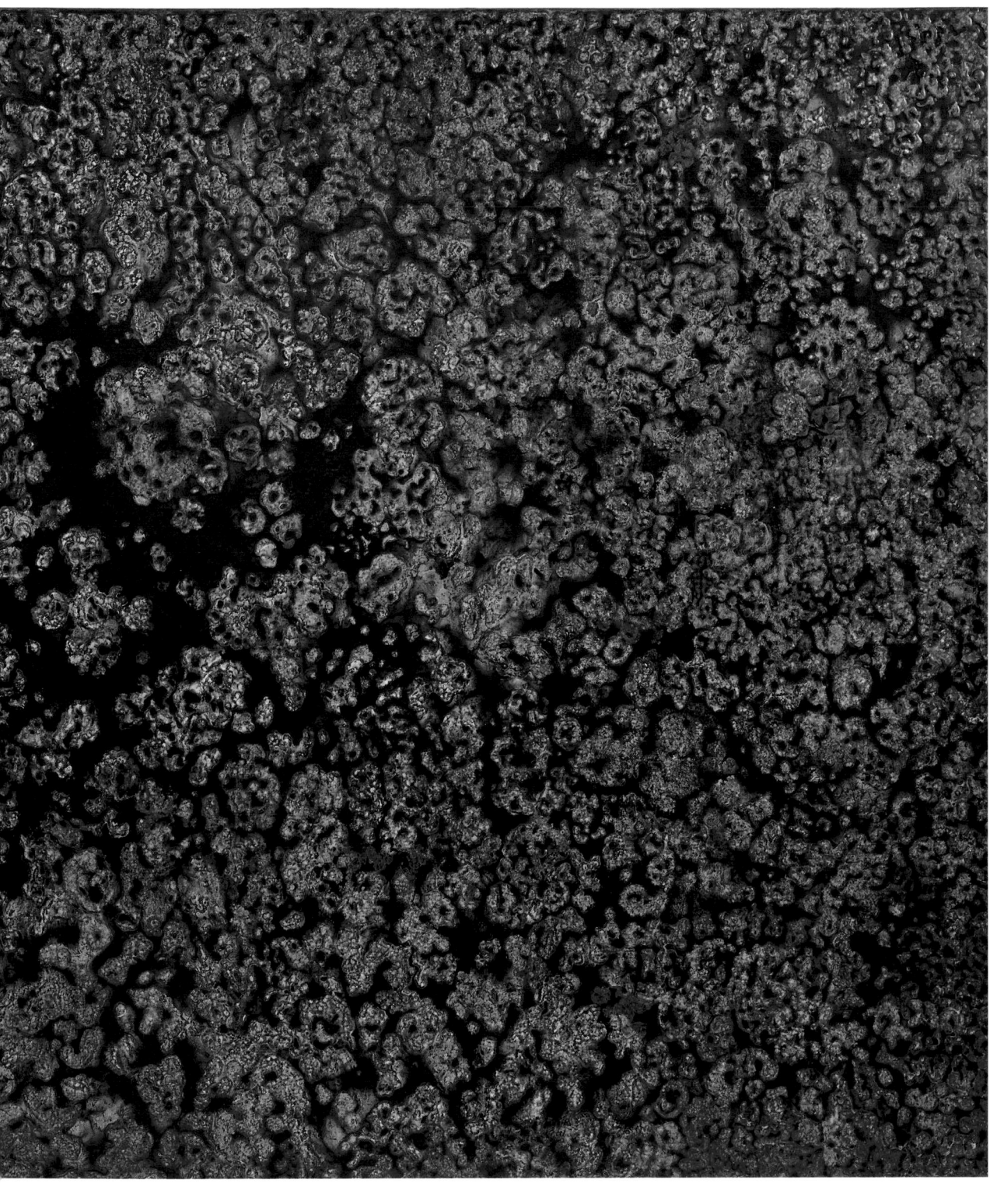

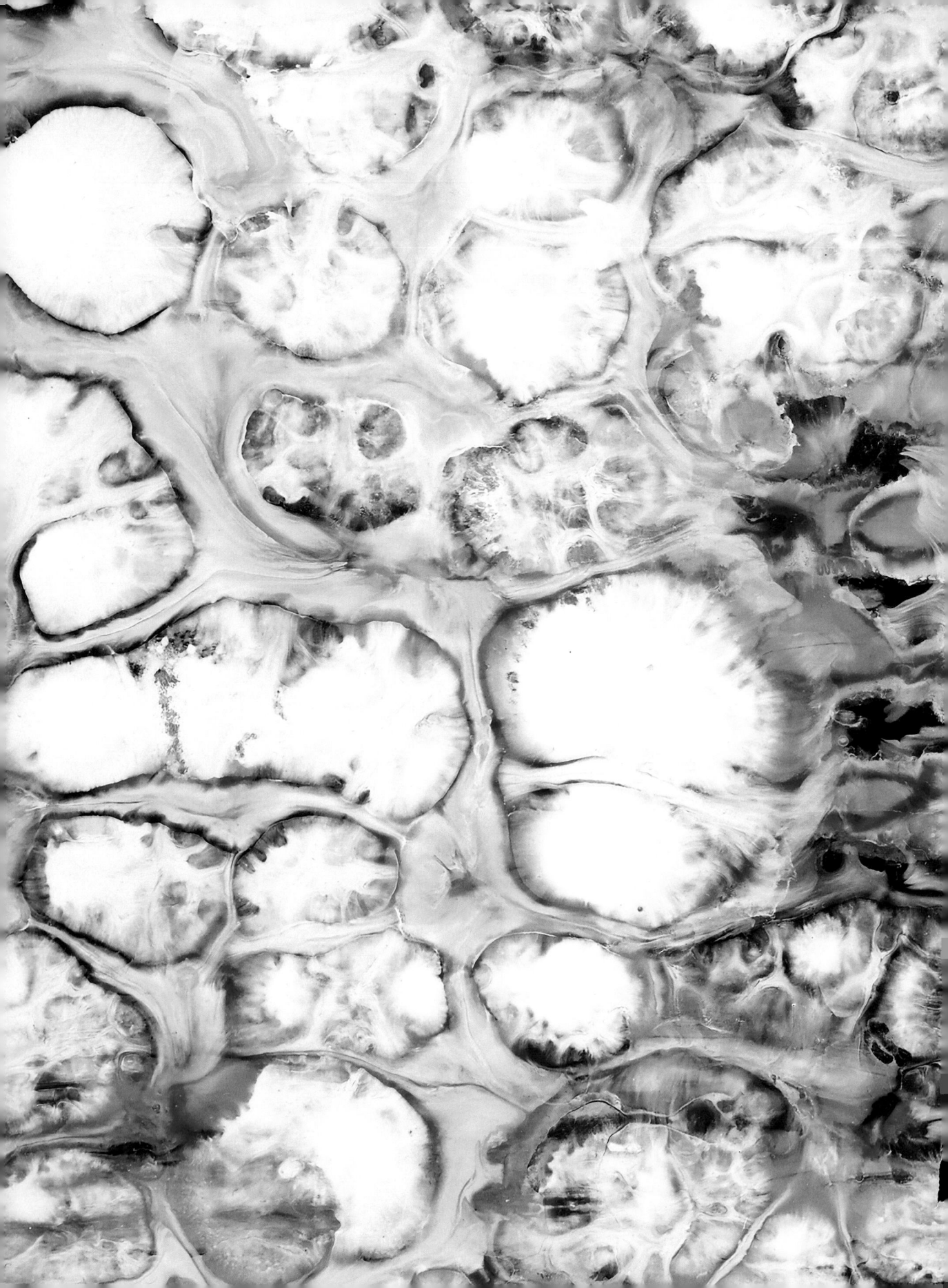

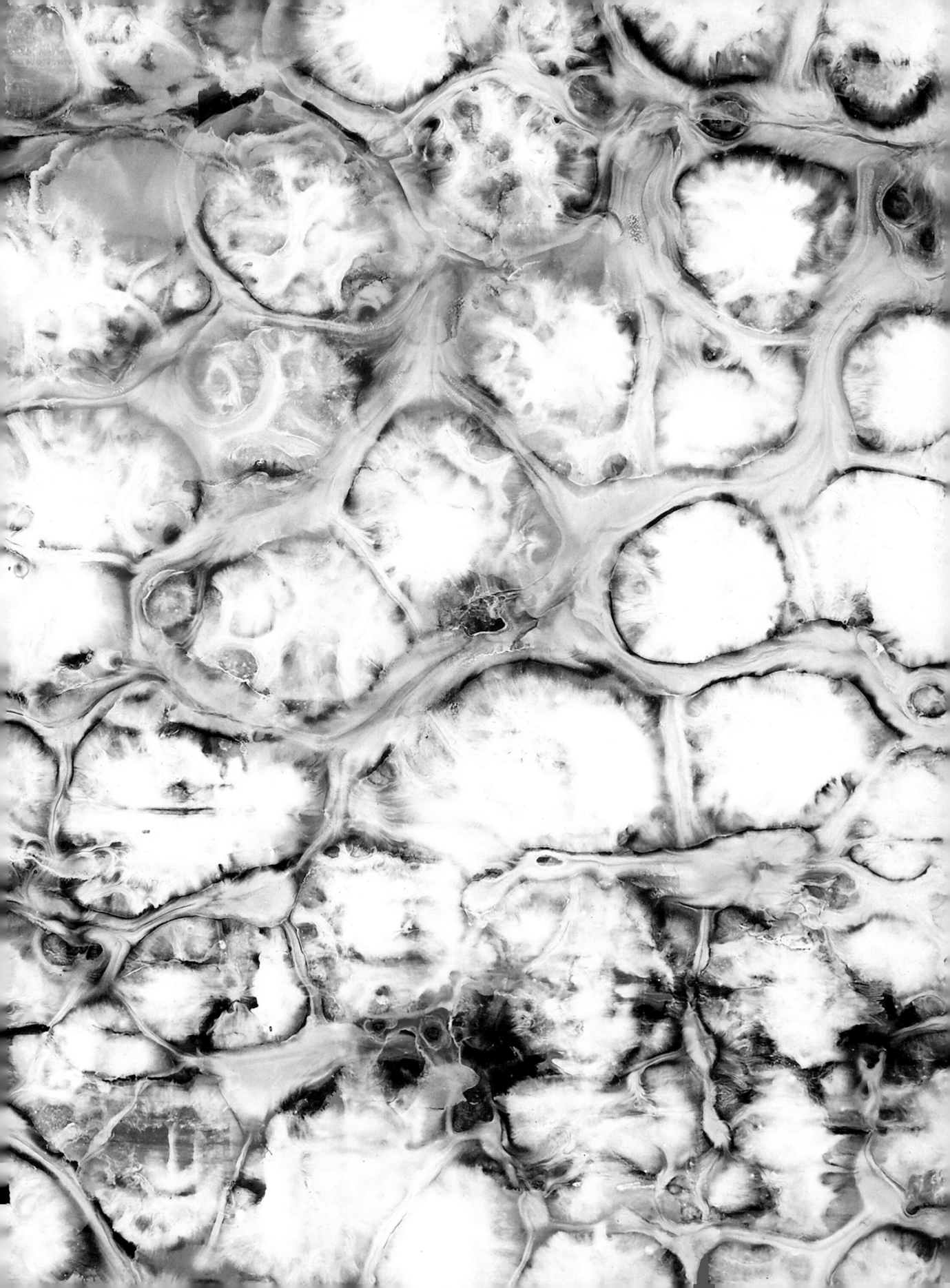

# Karen Barth

## Individual Exhibitions

2005    Cheryl Pelavin Fine Art, New York, New York
2002    Cheryl Pelavin Fine Art, New York, New York
1997    Doyle Gallery, San Francisco, California
1994    Galerie Hauser, Frankfurt, Germany
1985    Hunter College Art Gallery, New York, New York,
          "MFA Thesis Show"

## Group Exhibitions

2005    Elliot Smith Contemporary Art, New York, New York,
          "Master Prints"
2005    The Tate Chelsea, New York, New York,
          "Backing into Landscape"
2003    Ethan Cohen Fine Arts, New York, New York,
          "Redo China"
2000    Ethan Cohen Fine Arts, New York, New York,
          "Provincetown Workshop Benefit"
1998    James Graham and Sons, New York, New York,
          "Karen Barth, David Mann and Thomas Martinelli"
1997    James Graham and Sons, New York, New York,
          "Landscape as Abstraction"
1996    Larry Kahn Gallery, Kansas City, Missouri,
          "Abstraction From New York"
1994    Edward Thorp Gallery, New York, New York,
          "Paint Royale"
1994    Edward Thorp Gallery, New York, New York,
          "Summer Group Show"
1988    Silvermine Guild, New Cannan, Connecticut,
          "39th Art of the Northeast Competition,"
          curated by Lowery Sims (Associate Curator of 20th Century Art,
          Metropolitan Museum, New York City)
1986    Pleides Gallery, New York, New York,
          "Against the Grain," curated by Peter Plagens
1985    Hunter College Art Gallery, New York, New York,
          "MFA Exhibition"

pages 80–81
*M.A.P.P. #1h* (detail)
2001
Polymer on wood,
16" x 20"

82

## Bibliography

ART in Embassies Program Catalogue, United States Mission to the North Atlantic Treaty Organization, Brussels, 2006

*The New York Times*: Karen Barth, Cheryl Pelavin Fine Art by Ken Johnson, September 27, 2002

*Dreams: 1900–2000, Science, Art, and the Unconscious Mind*, edited by Lynn Gamwell, Cornell University Press, 2000

*The New York Times*: Karen Barth, David Mann and Thomas Martinelli by Ken Johnson, January, 1998

*Review Magazine*: Karen Barth, David Mann and Thomas Martinelli by Robert Murdock, December, 1997

*Art News:* "Landscape as Abstraction" by Carol Diehl, June, 1997

For further information regarding Karen Barth's work, go to karenbarth.com or contact the archive at karenbarth.archive@gmail.com.

cover
**Winter** (detail)
2014
Archival pigment
on paper, mounted
on panel, 40" x 80"